HOME
BY THE RIVER

HOME
BY THE RIVER

by

Archibald Rutledge

Illustrated with Photographs
by Noble Bretzman

The Bobbs-Merrill Company
Publishers
INDIANAPOLIS   NEW YORK

PRINTED IN THE UNITED STATES OF AMERICA
BY THE CORNWALL PRESS, CORNWALL, N. Y.

To
ALICE LUCAS RUTLEDGE,
loving comrade
in all my Hampton adventures

For courteous permission to reprint certain of the material in this book, the author makes grateful acknowledgment to the editors of *The Saturday Evening Post*.

CONTENTS

HOME
BY THE RIVER

Chapter 1
The Native Returns

WHEN in August, 1937, I returned to Hampton, the road was almost closed by a lush growth of grass and briars and bushes. When I came to where the gate used to be, I could hardly see the house for the tall weeds and the taller bushes. It was as if the blessing of fecundity had been laid on everything natural, and on everything human, the curse of decay. Yet when I drove up to the house, there were seven Negroes, a loyal if tattered company, to meet me. They said little, but I could feel their affection and their eagerness to help. What better encouragement could any man have who is making any kind of difficult start?

At the age of fifty-six, after an absence of forty-four years, I returned to the country where I was born, with a desire to restore this 209-year-old house, and a property that has been in my family since 1686. I purposed also to beautify the grounds so that the place would have loveliness as an attraction as well as its natural deep historic significance. Hampton Plantation, in the coastal country of South Carolina, forty miles northeast of Charleston, is the ancient home of my ancestors; and because, since my return, so many adventures have befallen me, I believe it worth while to record them. There is a theory that those who gamble can't win, but the fact of the matter is that those who do not gamble can't win. Whatever be the undertaking, we always have to leave a good deal to chance.

[13]

It was assuredly so when I decided to return to Hampton to live. That it was a foolhardy thing to attempt, practically all my friends warned me. Deserted plantations in the Carolinas are usually bought by millionaires, who turn them into magnificent estates, often surpassing in beauty the originals. Whatever work had to be done at Hampton, I had to do largely myself. But perhaps half the fun in the venture has come from that very fact. I always liked the saying, "The difficult is what can be done now; the impossible, what can be done soon."

People have often asked me how, in the first place, I ever found it possible to leave Hampton. I never left it of my own free will. But my parents felt that their exceedingly rural plantation son had urgent need of the disciplines of education and contact with civilization. Accordingly, when I was thirteen years old, and a yearling in every sense of the word, I was lassoed and sent to school in Charleston. Here there were scholarships for poor Southern boys who wanted to go to Northern colleges. The scholarships were good when parents wanted their boy to attend college and the boy did not. Such was my case. In the year 1900 I went to Union. Upon my graduation in 1904 I took up newspaper work in Washington. One day early in the autumn of that year I received a wire from the headmaster of Pennsylvania's famous Mercersburg Academy, asking me if I could come up for two weeks to take the place of a teacher who was ill. I soon discovered that the man was not ill, but the headmaster was sick of him. He was fired; and I, who had come to stay a few days, remained for thirty-three years. Life is often like that.

The place to which I returned is justly famous, though I have done nothing to make it so. The two-thousand-acre tract lying on the southern bank of the Santee, which few people realize is the largest river of the eastern United States, has been in my family since Daniel Horry, one of my Huguenot ancestors, fled from France at the time of the Revocation of the Edict of Nantes. It is ten miles up the river from the ocean, and lies just off the Coastal Highway. I have a map of the place, done in color with meticulous care, by the earliest owners. The date of this plat is 1702. Here will be a spot designated as "ye little gumm tree." Here will be another, with the legend, "ye antient cypress tree." Those Huguenots were good colonists and good neighbors; and one thing that made them so was the care they always took in the matter of their property lines.

Before entering into an account of my many adventures at Hampton during the last four years, it seems wise to give some idea of the nature and the lore of the country to which I returned.

In parts of our ample land the possibilities in local history are almost exhausted. But in many regions of the far South, once so well known and once of so great national importance, the records of the past are now as spiritually veiled as they are materially by the gray mystery of the Spanish moss that shrouds the live oaks and the yellow pines. Here, but especially in my Santee country, one comes upon the allurement of beauty's reticence and shadowy avoidance, the haunting charm of the inaccessible. Through this historic land of dreams and memories every year pass hundreds of thousands of visitors. They do not want to miss anything, especially anything that has about it authentic romance. They do not want to pass Glamour at sixty miles an hour. It is here, but not really visible. From it the arras must be drawn aside in order that the meaning and the mystery may be both revealed and understood.

Three hundred miles away, far in the tawny-maned sea breakers of the western North Carolina mountains, rise those streams that form, in the sister state to the southward, the Wateree and Congaree Rivers. These, uniting not far below Columbia, the capital of South Carolina and a city in almost the geometric center of the state, form the mighty Santee, which flows eastward for more than a hundred miles to the coast.

It is a river of vast volume, bearing down silt in a manner that makes it resemble the Nile; like the Nile's, also, are the Santee's periodic floods. When it is in freshet, I have known it to rise more than fifteen feet at my plantation; and, near its mouth, to attain a width of five miles. It is navigable almost to Columbia. The Santee should be in the public eye just now; for this great river, draining one of the major watersheds of the East, is, for hydro-political purposes, going to be utterly destroyed. Sixty miles from its mouth it is going to be diverted into the little Cooper, a mere wood stream, which empties into Charleston harbor. From the dam to the ocean there will be no more river. But that is a story of the present, while mine is of the past.

Sixteen miles from its mouth, the Santee divides; and these two streams flow independently into the ocean. Between them is the lonely delta of the Santee, formerly one of the greatest rice-growing areas of North America, but now returned to a green wilderness as primeval as it must have been in the days of the Indians. Once under a high state of cultivation, it is now the semi-tropical haunt of wild boars, deer, alligators, wild turkeys and myriads of wild fowl. In fact, it is one of the great American Rivieras for migrated ducks. This delta, from one to three miles wide throughout its length, was an integral part of every plantation that lay across either branch of the river from it. Each planter would have from two to three thousand acres of upland and pineland, and then a holding of the delta, usually from a hundred to a thousand acres. Even when I was a boy, most of these fields were planted; and I have, as a cherished recollection, the vision of a glorious field of a thousand acres of rice, level and golden, stretching between the two broad rivers toward the sea.

Within the memory of men still living almost a score of great plantations throve on the southern bank of the river, and there were eight or ten on the northern shore. On the South Santee, inhabited or but recently deserted, I remember Waterhon, Wambaw, my own Hampton, Romney, Montgomery, Peafield, Peachtree, Fairfield, Palo Alto, the Wedge, Harrietta, Woodville, Egremont, Mazyck's and Washoe. There were homes also on Murphy's Island and on Cedar Island, at the mouth of the river. Ormond Hall was near by. Of all these great plantations, Hampton alone is occupied by its original owners; Fairfield is still owned by the Pinckneys, but it is not occupied.

I must say a word about those rice fields on the delta because the owners appear to have had a personal feeling and affection for each one. Not only were the plantations named, and usually with appropriate picturesqueness, but each field had its name and took on the quality of a personality. Those old planters, taking over a wilderness, devised for their posterity the empire of the earth; but it was as impossible for them as it is for any of us to control the future. Yet they did leave us a heritage of poetic names. To be able to refer to a field by name instantly identified it, so that directions about the work in it could be given explicitly, and could be immediately apprehended. I remember Jackfield where as a lad I caught a record bull alligator; Norman, White Oak, Lone Pine, Wampee, Broad Ditch, Daisyland, Eagle's Nest, Rice Queen. I have seen a map of the plantation fields done all in color by their owner, with each field named, and with a record of the field's yield year after year.

The Negro is especially susceptible to the magic of names, and he responds quickly to the stimulus of friendly rivalry. As he is not equally stimulated to work by much else, the old planters used to get their Negroes excited over the relative merits of various fields. There was some personal interest in hearing that White Oak had surpassed Norman in yield, and that Fanny had been less prolific this year than Talullah.

Far down the delta, near Midland, Moorland, Mottefield, and Tranquillity, there still stand what are perhaps the strangest buildings in North America. That region of the coast was, in 1822, visited by a dreadful tropical storm. During that hurricane several white overseers, one plantation owner and a great many Negro slaves were drowned in the rice fields near the mouth of the river. In order to establish places of refuge in case such a storm should come again, so-called slave towers were built. These were circular structures of brick, resembling miniature lighthouses. Rising out of the lone and level stretches of those immense lowlands, they are weird, almost inhuman, towers; and the real purpose of their being has given rise to endless conjecture. They suggest dungeons and tortures; but they were built solely as refuges in time of tornado.

When I was a small boy, I knew an old lady who was then over ninety years old. She remembered the fearful gale of 1822; and when we had hurricanes (there were disastrous ones in 1893 and in 1916), she would just sniff. She had been through the Great Gale.

The delta was not only laid out beautifully for planting, but the rice crop demanded that this whole area should be ditched and banked. At the canal heads were trunks, which controlled the height of water in the fields. It is tidewater country and although the ocean is so near, the salt water never enters far enough into the rivers to affect the rice growing. The fields could be flooded or drained on the flow or ebb of the tide.

Not long ago I had a strange experience on the extreme western tip of the delta, where I was hunting wild turkeys. Apparently primeval, with immense canebrakes, gloomy swamps and towering trees, this great swampland, I was amazed to discover, gave definite evidence that it had once been under close cultivation. At regular intervals were the ancient canals; here were the old banks, in many cases almost intact; and, strangest of all, here were the cypress trunks, no longer fulfilling their office, but still in place and still sound. This is a haunted region, for there is no earthly loneliness like that created by man's abandonment of what he once loved, enjoyed and considered secure and permanent.

Besides what we might call the agricultural remains, there are evidences on the delta of other human occupation. The Indians camped on the high sandy hillocks, and on Indian Hill there are a good many mounds. These, however, appear to be kitchen middens rather than sepulchers. There was a much later occupancy than even the rice-planting period. During the time of the noble experiment of prohibition, I suppose there was no region of all North America more favorable to the illicit distiller than the Santee delta. During my periodic visits in those days, I used to be able to stand on the back porch of my plantation house and hear the intriguingly unlawful sounds of stills being built in those marshy wastelands bordering the river. To make a good still, a man must have a firm foundation (not moral); wherefore these elusive gentry used to visit by night the once stately homes and from their ruins steal the fine old English bricks for their modern illegal purposes. Today, if I want massive and historic bricks, all I have to do is to paddle in my boat to the sites of these abandoned stills. I have found some bricks that I have been unable to classify: they are of great age, are thin, delicately fluted on both sides and have four holes drilled through them. Lying long on the riverbanks, most of these bricks become covered with vivid green moss, so that when they are used to edge garden paths they are decorative as well as useful.

Thos. Lynch, Jr.

Of the plantations that are contiguous to the lower Santee, those whose fame has come down to us have not owed
their renown to their size or to their richness, but rather to
some association with a famous personage. This is a heartening truth; for it suggests to us that, then as now, a spiritual
quality alone has in it the unfading vigor of immortality.
Only at such shrines can we who come after light the lonely
candles of our lives. Thus Hopseewee on the North Santee,
within sight of the Coastal Highway, owes its distinction
to the fact that it was the birthplace of Thomas Lynch, Jr.,
youngest of the signers of the Declaration. He was then
twenty-six years old. Edward Rutledge was but twenty-
seven. What responsibilities young men assumed in those
days! In signing that Declaration they jeopardized their
lives and their fortunes. Hopseewee House is still standing; for more than a century it has been owned by the
Lucas family. Outside of Magnolia Gardens I know of no
camellia japonicas so fragrant and beautiful as those at
Hopseewee.

Almost immediately across the river and the delta from
this place is the historic ruin of Peachtree, the home from
which the youngest signer journeyed with his bride to
Charleston, only a few years after he affixed his signature
to our immortal charter of liberty. The vessel on which
they voyaged toward Cuba was lost with all on board. The
house at Peachtree was burned about the year 1840; yet
after a century, the ends of some of the huge yellow pine
timbers, mortised in the brick walls, are still sound. You
can see where the fire charred their outer ends. The ruin
of this house is remarkably preserved: the high brick walls,

the gaping windows, through which huge trees have now grown, the massive granite steps, the iron balustrades. Formerly, in the very center of the middle cellar, there was a mysterious well of weird aspect and dreadful depth. As a boy, I remember seeing a young man at a picnic, bent on impressing his prowess on the girls present, run and jump over this black chasm. In precariously landing, he dislodged a brick from the lip of the moldering structure, the top of which was flush with the ground. It fell; and all of us breathlessly waited, listening. Finally came the deep subterranean splash that told that it had finally reached the water, suggesting also the abysmal depth of the hole. All through that country there are underground rivers that steal through passages in the rock by which the land is underlaid. No doubt this well tapped one of those streams. So many cattle and hogs, allured by the smell of the water from the well, plunged into it and perished that, some years ago, it was filled in with bricks from the place.

Far less impressive than this ruin and likely to be passed by, yet of more romantic human interest, is the low conical mound in the woods a half mile to the southward. The story of this mound is both tragic and appealing. More than a century ago a Spanish ship came sailing up the broad reaches of the South Santee, and one day cast anchor off Peachtree. A sick man was brought ashore, and the request was made that he be left there until the vessel's return from Charleston. The patient was young, handsome and an officer. The owner of Peachtree, who lived there with his only daughter, a lovely girl of eighteen, gladly gave the stranger sanctuary, and the daughter undertook to nurse him. But he had yellow fever, and within three days he was dead. The vessel never returned.

Ten days after the sailor's death the daughter was stricken, and she soon died. Then her father lost his mind. He barricaded the house. With his own hands he laid out his daughter for burial, and with his own hands he built her coffin. During the daytime he stood off sympathetic neighbors with a shotgun. In the deep of night, with the primordial strength of a maniac, he carried the coffin far into the heart of a fragrant thicket, set it upright on the surface of the ground, and heaped earth over it to a height of fifteen feet. When I was a child, this grave was about ten feet high; now it has sunk much lower. Out of the apex of this sacred pyramid grows a beautiful young pine, a fit symbol of immortality.

At the south end of the long Santee bridge, and visible from it, is Fairfield, the famous home of the Pinckneys. High on a tremendous bluff above the river its white porch looks out across the tide and across the glimmering delta fields, seeming indeed to be gazing forever out over the languorous spiritual autumn of the past. Although two miles away from the route of the old King's Highway, Fairfield was the object of especial persecution in the days of the Revolution, chiefly because those two renowned American rebels, Thomas and Charles Cotesworth Pinckney, called it home.

Just down the river from Fairfield stands the Wedge, famous for its beauty, its lovely gardens and its idyllic charm; famous also as having been built by William Lucas, the son of that English genius who invented and built the first American rice mill, which had the same effect on rice growing as Whitney's gin had on cotton. Within sight of the Wedge is Harrietta, about the building of which an extraordinary story can be told.

My great-great-grandmother, Harriott Horry, was then the mistress of "Hampton," my present home. It did not seem to her likely that her daughter, Harriott, would ever marry. Her mother therefore decided to create for her a real interest in life by building for her a home of her own, calling it "Harrietta." No love and no money were spared in the building of this beautiful house. With the affectionate and meticulous care characteristic of French Huguenots, the gardens were planted, some of them with bulbs imported from Holland. But just before the house was completed, Harriott eloped! And she went to live in Charleston. For some sixty years this lovely place stood deserted. Just before the Civil War it was purchased by the Doar family, who restored it and planted its magnificent camellias. Some ten years ago it passed into the possession of Mr. and Mrs. Horatio Shonnard. They have made Harrietta one of the most beautiful places in all the Deep South.

In Harrietta House I have seen what appealed to me as a priceless historic relic: it is a battered little notebook, smudged and dog-eared; but it is the roster of Marion's Men, those valiant patriot bushwhackers who made life miserable for the British regulars. Many of the descendants of those backwoods patriots are now living not ten miles from where their forebears used to make Redcoat uniforms look like sieves.

All the great houses built in that plantation region in the old days were erected slowly, painstakingly, with a certain massive grace. We have no record of their architects—if, indeed, there were any. They appear to have been planned by their owners, who, by affection more than by money, wrought out their dreams in enduring brick, marble, granite, black cypress, mahogany and yellow pine. A prodigious amount of mahogany was used, and it no doubt was brought in ballast from San Domingo. Here and there one finds exquisite hand-carving. Some of this was done in England; but much of it was done by Negro slaves.

We are often predisposed to think that the only wilderness conquered in this country was the wilderness west of the Mississippi. But the whole East was once primeval forest; and the Carolina wilds, because of their semi-tropical nature, must have been almost impenetrable. The genius of the French and English for colonizing was never better displayed than in the opening up of the gross hinterlands that lay on three sides of Charleston.

The setting for the delightful life of culture of the plantations was romantic and picturesque to an extraordinary degree. There were the immense tracts of woods, timbered with virgin pine and oak, ash and hickory; dark, misty, forbidding swamps, the haunts of many wild and some savage creatures; rivers, difficult to navigate and hard to bridge; sunny shrubberies of a tropical luxuriance of growth; solitary reaches of melancholy coastline; vast stretches of delta lands, as rich as Egypt. Nowhere else in the world has nature been kinder to her children than in those regions where the great plantations were formed out of the Eden-like wilderness of the Low Country. And that charm is an eternal one; though the civilization that it cradled and nourished has passed away, the charm survives. The home remains lovely after the guests are gone.

Chapter 2
Social Life at Hampton

CERTAIN writers have invested plantation life with glamour. I believe it had that glamour. Other writers have insisted that plantation glamour was a myth. I think they are wrong. Those ills which are incident to life everywhere are mentioned as occurring on plantations in the Deep South, and are offered as a proof that romance did not exist. I never can understand why a romanticist thinks he is wholly right, nor why a realist thinks he is. Both are right and both are wrong. Life everywhere, in all ages, has its azaleas and has its razorbacks. But the moonlight of life is as authentic as its sunlight.

I have learned about the social life on the plantations in the old days, and more recently, from books; from family history, which is preserved in letters; from tradition (which usually is an admixture of fact and fancy); from conversations with very old and keenly observant people; and from my own recollections, which, of course, do not extend back further than fifty years.

In general it may be asserted with absolute truth that at Hampton, and on all plantations like it, there was a social intercourse as gentle and as refined as ever existed in America. People were enamoured with the art of living. They enthroned honor; and as Edmund Burke says of them, they felt a stain like a wound.

[27]

I suppose that no clearer indication of the culture of a people can be found than that disclosed by an examination of their reading matter. There has always been at Hampton an unusual library, not so large as it is distinctive. The oldest book I have is Sir Edward Coke's *Laws of England*, printed in 1590. Practically all the French classics, especially those of the eighteenth century, are there, including Voltaire, Racine, Corneille, Montesquieu. There are no German books; but there are first editions of practically everything worth while in English from the time of Milton. There is a magnificent Johnson's edition of Shakespeare. I get the impression that the early colonists of a certain station had in England standing orders for anything significant in a literary way. There are ornate sets of sermons, especially those of Hale, Burnet and Tollotson.

One day I was examining a set of these sermons, which, to tell the truth, did not seem to have been much read, when I found, hidden behind them, a little dog-eared volume, read almost ragged. It was Boccaccio's *Decameron*! Someone had, long ago, hidden it behind the sermons, feeling that no more safe hiding place could be found.

The first editions include those of Tennyson, Browning, Dickens and Thackeray. One day I found an autographed copy of Florence Nightingale's *Autobiography*. Few people, I believe, know that she ever wrote one.

Books on law, on religion, on politics, on history, poetry, drama and fiction of the highest type—these constituted the reading of plantation families. And it was this sort of education, together, perhaps, with schooling in England, which enabled a young man like Thomas Lynch, Jr., to affix his signature to the Declaration of Independence when he was only twenty-six years old. As a matter of fact, all four signers from South Carolina had been educated in England and were graduates of the Middle Temple Law School in London. As students there it is probable that they were associated with such men as Edmund Burke and Charles Fox, with William Blackstone and Charles Wyndham.

Burke commented on the Americans' fondness for law and, he added with his usual felicity, "This study renders men acute, inquisitive, dextrous, prompt in attack, ready in defence, full of resources."

The plantations of the Carolina Low Country had what might be termed a double social life; that is, there was the social life among the various plantations; then there was the social life in Charleston. For Charleston was always the social capital of the plantations. It was customary for the plantation owners, who spent much of their time at the seashore, abroad, or in the mountains in the summer, to return to their winter homes after the first heavy frosts, which in that region come toward the middle of November. About the first of the year, the young society people repaired to Charleston for the season of gaiety and mirth, which always ended abruptly with the beginning of Lent.

You will notice that I do not speak of these social customs as belonging only to Hampton; they were not peculiar to one plantation, but were the customs of the country. And these customs underwent practically no change from colonial days until the unhappy year of 1860. A traveler from Europe in 1800 thus speaks of Charleston:

"In no other part of the globe is hospitality so much practised as in Charleston. . . . A Carolinian, though not very opulent, rarely has less than twenty servants in attendance on his table, his stables, his kitchen. There are few families that do not keep a chaise or a coach, and ladies rarely set foot on the streets. The manner of living is nearly the same as in England. . . . The ladies are extremely temperate, and generally drink water; the gentlemen are sober and industrious."

We learn also from contemporaneous descriptions that Shakespeare was often played in the city; that the importation of the best French and English furniture, of silks and satins and broadcloth, of jewels and of ornaments of gold went on rather lavishly; to such a degree, indeed, as to lead one visitor to record, "I should hardly know that I was not in London or Paris."

The entertainments in the great country homes, on the plantations, those homes of which Hampton is a typical example, were irregular; but in many respects they were as elaborate as those in the city. The reasons for this were simple: there was abundant domestic help; venison and wild turkeys and wild ducks were almost always to be had; and the general feeling for entertainment was perhaps higher in the country than in the city. Perhaps nowhere else was hospitality considered almost a religious rite. Much of the entertaining was of strangers and travelers over the long woodland roads. Apparently anyone who came was welcomed. Nor did this feeling of responsibility toward travelers cease with the passing of the splendor of plantation life. When I was a little boy, I wandered one day into the pantry, bent on despoliation, but assuming an elaborate air of innocence. Our Negro cook, old Martha, apprehended me just as I was reaching for something good.

"Don't you take dat!" she told me with unwonted severity; "don't you ever take nothin' from de Unexpected Company Shelf."

Not infrequently visitors were members of the family who came to spend not a week end but a winter's end. I recall many such relatives at Hampton; they were, in the best sense, members of the family; they helped with the housekeeping, tried to lighten burdens, told us stories of life in the city, read us endless English classics. I should say that, before the Civil War, there were not a great many formal entertainments on any of the plantations; but there was constant readiness to dispense a profuse and heartfelt hospitality. Now and then there would be a wedding reception, a ball or a dinner party for some famous visitor like Washington or Jefferson. However, three distinct forms of country entertainment deserve to be remembered.

On no other estates in America has wild game always been so abundant as on the Carolina plantations. And from colonial times one way for a plantation owner to entertain his guests was by deer hunting—riding to hounds, after the English fashion. In the forests of the Low Country, at least before the days of turpentine, the level floors of the woods afforded ideal riding; and following the hounds on horseback was a romantic and exciting sport.

[31]

Great pride was taken in the quality both of the horses and the hounds; and plantation owners vied with one another in having packs of hounds the voices of which were matched like chiming bells. In present days privileged guests usually are invited to shoot ducks or quail; but in an elder day deer hunting was considered the aristocrat of sports. Even now, in woods like those of Hampton, grand deer hunting is to be had.

A second rather distinctive sport was horse racing. On several of the great roads approaching Charleston there were racecourses of a mile or more laid out; and throughout the cooler months of the year the gentry were wont to gather at these for their hardy recreation. Jockeys were rarely employed, since the owners themselves raced their favorite horses.

A third recreation that belonged distinctively to the plantations was the custom of journeying by water to visit one's neighbors. Although both the roads and carriages were usually dubious in their efficiency, the river rolled by all the plantations of my country. Much was made of boats; and many Negro slaves had no other employment than that of oarsmen. I remember going to a wedding in a rather stately barge that had a high prow that curved backward. My dusky oarsmen might well have been Nubians; I certainly felt like Marc Antony, and the girl with me looked, I thought, like Cleopatra.

For the beauty of the life that our ancestors enjoyed on these great estates in the country, it was essential that there should have been foundations of deep and authentic character. Of these, religion was unquestionably the first.

They lived in a day before many sects had ravaged the land. The faith of the French Huguenots, in consonance with that of the people of the Church of England, strengthened the already sterling quality of the planters. The temper and character of the English Cavaliers and the Huguenots were singularly congenial. Alike in their sensitiveness to beauty, to the appeals of chivalry and the nobler instincts, to an unwritten code of honor, they naturally became affectionate friends and neighbors. Surrounded by the wilderness, theirs was sometimes a pioneer existence; but it was never a mean one.

The people of the coastal parishes took their religion seriously; yet with great good sense they did not permit it to interfere with their domestic comfort. On fair Sundays the old coaches that drove down the pineland roads carried heavy hampers as well as sin-burdened hearts. After service, communal dinners were held at a respectful distance from the church.

One of the most beautiful of the parish churches of early America is St. James, Santee (built about 1760). Beautiful and solitary, surrounded by the wildwoods, it stands beside the King's Highway. In the old days this church was the gathering place for the whole wide rural community; and the careful observer will notice the name of Thomas Lynch written on the back of one of the pews. They came in coaches and carriages; in "chariots," as some said, but the young blades always rode their thoroughbreds. It is significant that the road north of the church is, even today, singularly straight, wide and level for a distance of two miles. It was one of the parish colonial racecourses, and the legend is that both to and from church the gay sparks of those days used to race their horses. This ancient church, with its circular brick pillars, its high-backed cypress pews, its massive pulpit and communion rail of San Domingo mahogany, and its indefinable air of austere sanctity, is now open once a year for worship, on the second Sunday in April; and the descendants of former parishioners come from far and near to attend this annual service.

But I had intended to tell more of the social life at Hampton, and how its ease and grace were made possible. One may get ideas about much of this from the furnishings of a house; for wherever there is material elegance, there is the record of some effort in the direction of culture, of hospitality, of a generous recognition of the importance of living—or rather of the importance of the art of living.

One is impressed at Hampton by the number of tables, each one of which had its social use; bedside tables, massive ones with great marble tops for serving; delicate rosewood tables; spacious ones of walnut and San Domingo mahogany. There is the mahogany table from which Washington dined; and there is a much older table, circular, probably a dining table, of native black walnut. This table clearly shows the hand-planing of two hundred years ago. In one of the upper rooms there is a table of ebony. In the hall is a drop leaf of curly maple. Unquestionably, some of this furniture was made on the plantation. Certain pieces, unique in design, are now being reproduced.

In the great master bedroom, the ceiling of which goes up two stories, the room occupying the western wing of the house and corresponding to the ballroom on the east, there are several huge mahogany wardrobes and dressers. The boards out of which they are made are solid, are singularly wide and are comparatively thin. Much of the wood is burly, but there has been no attempt made to get sunburst effects; indeed, this usually can be done only with veneers. Perhaps the most interesting feature of these pieces of furniture is their hinges, all solid brass, delicate yet strong, and all of original design. One set of hinges particularly attracts me: they are like big maple leaves, one opening over the other.

One heirloom that constantly wins favor for itself is a most elaborately hand-carved mirror, of solid mahogany. It was the work of some forgotten Negro slave. Remarkable as it may seem, the carving on the two sides and that on the top and on the bottom are entirely different; that is, considering that it has four sides, all have a different design. But the effect is harmonious. That dusky artist of the long ago achieved the unity and the authentic beauty that comes from blending, with an artist's wizard touch, divergent elements.

I have found a wrought-iron brazier for heating a coach. The lion-head handles and the feet are silver. It suggests that a journey to church or the long trip of forty miles to Charleston, while not what we should consider streamlined, yet was made with some attention to the details of elegance and comfort.

Of musical instruments in Hampton (some have been removed) I do have a very ancient organ; and, in the spacious attic, what appears to be a harp, homemade, but

with elaborate carving of the woodwork. Although I cannot play a harp here (nor shall be able to do so hereafter),
I purpose to restore this interesting relic.

Surrounded as I am by these material evidences of social
significance, it is not difficult for me to imagine the quiet,
orderly, generous-hearted life of the plantation. I have a
record that the rice crop would sometimes net as much
as twenty thousand dollars a year; and that was in days
when a dollar was worth a dollar. When people have an
income like that, and are socially inclined, they can live
as they wish. Although vulgarity is often an attendant of
wealth, on the plantations the vulgar and the ostentatious
were entirely absent. People who knew their Jeremy
Taylor, their Addison, their Molière, their Montesquieu,
their Gibbon and their Voltaire were not inclined to make
social spectacles of themselves.

Chapter 3
The Valley of Decision

IN RETURNING to the country where I was born I would, I knew, be coming back to the scenes and memories of my childhood where many adventures had befallen me. A mention of a few of them may explain why, though I was happy during the years I was in the North—and was gently transplanted—I never took root.

I began hunting when I was six years old, and when I was nine, I killed my first stag. Responsibilities were put on plantation boys early. By the time I was ten, I had much to do with riding the woods after stock; and one of my special tasks was to discover and to care for expectant mothers among the cows, goats and hogs. Most children of the city hear of birth and death as strange rumors, but I saw them soon and their aspect filled me with an abiding sense of the mystery of life. Close calls I had with savage bulls and steers, with alligators and huge diamondback rattlesnakes. I raised pet deer and raccoons, squirrels and mockingbirds. Riding a barebacked horse to school several miles each day through the wildwoods, I came to love and to study nature, to know something of the birds and the beasts, the trees and the flowers. Negroes were my daily companions, and from them I learned something of the ways of the natural world. Something of their attitude toward nature became mine.

I remember coming home one April twilight along the alluring yet forbidding margins of a fragrant wild thicket. There were three Negro men with me, all apparently ordinary in their powers of feeling, which should have been at a low ebb after the long sultry day we had spent looking at some cypress timber in the hot wilderness of a half-submerged swamp.

Our footfalls sounded lonely as we padded along, one after the other. Fading glory of sunset suffused the solitary woodlands. I had a sense of entering another world through those ponderous portals of the west. Suddenly I was aware that my humble comrades had paused behind me and were chanting something in unison. Turning, I saw them standing in a little group, each with hands clasped reverently, and as they gazed into the rose-tinted west they kept saying, as if softly intoning a prayer, "God bless the New Moon!"

They had seen more than I had and their reaction to what they saw was superior to mine. Far in the west hung the silvery sickle of the new moon. It marked, in its way, the beginning of a new month; and the Negroes, grimed and tired as they were, paused to bless God and to worship.

Ever since that evening of my boyhood days I have, with a deepening respect, noticed plantation Negroes performing this joyous mystic rite. Even little children in the midst of their last entrancing twilight frolic will, upon seeing the new moon gleaming in the heavens, pause in their play to look upward and, with hands suddenly clasped, say, "God bless the New Moon!" A moment later, their vespers done, they will again be breathlessly chasing one another, as children do at dusk.

Memories of the past, these have always haunted me and drawn me back toward the land I loved! I like to remember Prince Alston, my especial Negro comrade. Of the same age, we were close friends for forty-five years.

One day when we were boys, he was paddling me in a small cypress canoe in a lagoon. The channel was narrow, black and very deep. On either side were great beds of lily pads, beyond which were quaking emerald islands, and beyond these the swamplands. On these singular islands alligators are very fond of basking; for they are easy of access to the water and the big reptiles can regain their element readily from these floating couches.

I was fishing for bass, but I had a small gun in the canoe. As we rounded a bend in the stream an old bull alligator, a monster of this watery wilderness, roused himself from his siesta upon one of the green islands. Slightly raising his formidable head, he surveyed us in a sinister reptilian way. This attitude was unusual, for surprised by man, an alligator, however large he may be, usually makes a wild plunge for the water in which he submerges himself. But this individual just happened to be different. He gazed at us critically, a dull menace in his stony stare. Then he turned his massive bulk toward us, waiting in a kind of grim and huge defiance.

We were now quite near him, the buoyant canoe appearing indeed a frail thing beside his massive bulk. He looked black and terrible, reminding me of a battleship, and the stains of mud on his armored hide enhanced the grimness of his appearance. Prince, a skillful boatman, stayed the canoe's approach.

"Look out," he warned me.

Laying down my rod, I picked up my gun. But I was less interested in shooting the alligator than in discovering his intentions—the unusual in nature has always had for me an especial fascination. This old brute looked like a personality. He was not less than twelve feet long and in bulk he was tremendous.

What he meant to do he now proceeded to show us. He launched himself into the water with a grace and a swiftness surprising in a creature so ungainly. Instead of submerging he kept on the surface; and instead of trying to escape us he came head-on for us. He had all the appearance of a submarine running on the surface, intent upon ramming its victim. He could easily have upset the canoe or crushed it like an eggshell with his massive jaws. There was something fateful in his silent and purposeful approach.

Glancing back at Prince, I judged from the expression on his usually impassive face that he had never before been so interested in anything. The bull was now only twenty feet away, coming for us with a determination not to be misunderstood. He was going to try his brute strength against his ancient and inveterate enemy.

I had the gun leveled on his head. Not for a moment did he pause or waver in his course. He was coming fast, a dull rippling wave in the black water under his jaws. His steely unblinking eyes fixed us with a cold and sinister glare. Only a reptile has that peculiar look, one well calculated to chill and to awe.

When he was within six feet, I shot him. I waited too long; for in his gigantic death throes he almost upset us.

I hardly had any choice in the killing of this minotaur, and certainly no scruples about putting an end to the cruel reign of such a tyrant. He does great damage, and keeps in mortal dread nearly all the gentle and beautiful wild creatures that inhabit the region where he resides.

There was a notorious old bull alligator in Witch Pond, not far from our plantation house; he had for a certainty killed two calves, several hogs, one of our favorite hounds, and had created a reign of terror among the stock. About him and his depredations the Negroes had a kind of superstition, so that it was in vain that we tried to enlist their aid in ridding the plantation of this malignant brigand. The massive strength of such a creature can readily be imagined. His life is one long murderous career.

One thing that made an approach to this solitary monster difficult was the fact that Witch Pond was surrounded by dense thickets. Many an attempted stalk of mine was frustrated by the noise that I could not help making. This lone stretch of water was lazily drained by a shallow ditch that conducted the slight overflow through the woods to the distant river. One day I thought of a plan by which I could come upon the minotaur of Witch Pond: I decided to wade into it by way of the ditch, and in this manner silently to approach the monster that, during the heat of the day, had a habit of basking on an old cypress log half-submerged in the water.

By following the water route I reached the lagoon without making a sound, and as soon as a clear view of the place was afforded, I thrilled to see the vast and scaly bulk of the great reptile prone on the log that he had selected as his favorite haunt when he wanted to sun-bathe. Almost as soon as I saw him I realized that he was within rifle range; but there were many cypresses growing in the water, and some of these intervened between me and my intended prey. Besides, to kill an alligator, the shot should be made in the head or behind the foreshoulder, and neither vital spot was at first visible to me. The footing in the pond was none too good, for, although I was walking but a few feet from the shore, so soft was the bottom with its bubbling ooze of decayed leaves that the water was almost to my waist. At the time I was ten years old.

When an alligator is thus sunning himself, he is likely to be drowsing, so that if he hears nothing, he can be approached quite closely. It was so in this case. My slow progress through the water was without sound and in a few minutes the old marauder's whole body came clearly into view. And what a brute he was! Out of his element he appeared strangely naked and uncouth.

Just as I was raising my rifle I happened to glance back— more from instinct than for any definite reason. To my horror ten feet behind me lay a second alligator, even larger than the one on the log. I, the crafty stalker, had been stalked! In such a crisis one is not likely to remember everything. I recall feeling that I was at the mercy of this second alligator. I recall the slow turn I made, leveling my rifle on this grim submarine. Firing for his head at point-blank range, I dashed wildly and clumsily for the safety of the shore. Reaching the bank I turned to see what had happened. Over by the log where the first monster had been lying the waters were rocked into waves that he had started when he had plunged from the log at the report of the rifle. Near the shore, turning in blind circles, was my grim stalker. Another bullet put an end to him. Later we got him ashore, measured and weighed him. His weight was eleven hundred pounds and he was barely short of fourteen feet. His companion I caught on a line three years later and he had grown to even greater size.

Such a creature can easily kill a man, especially in the water, and despite much opinion to the contrary, I believe that under certain conditions he will do so. I hold this same conviction concerning certain sharks. They are not to be trusted. And I have always felt that on the day when that old U-boat followed me silently, it was for no good purpose.

When I was not playing with Prince and sharing with him all my hopes and fears, I was likely to be restlessly doing something-or-nothing. One spring evening after dinner while a pink and pearly afterglow still lingered behind the great live oaks and the tall pines that darkly and grandly fringed our western horizon, I ran out on the back porch; then, in that sheer abandon that belongs to a child's joyous spirit, I darted down the shrub-bordered pathway leading to Warsaw Creek which flows at a distance of some two hundred yards behind the house. It was dusky there in the twilight shadows, but the waters of the wide stream were brightened by the deep refulgence from the west. I had checked my speed somewhat and was about to turn back when I saw a small log lying across the dim pathway. I stepped upon it just to see if I could balance myself. I was barefooted at the time. Its bark felt curiously cold beneath my feet and it seemed to me that the log gave beneath my weight. But that I was standing on an entirely original kind of log was not borne home to me until my under-pinning began to move! It writhed. Then I heard a harsh and venomous hiss. Of course I deserted my perch in a flash and tore back up the path toward the kindly lights of the house. I was so scared that I told no one of my adventure.

The serpent must have been a very large one, either a cotton-mouth moccasin or a diamondback rattler, for no other snakes of that region grow to the size of my supposed log. What preserved me from being struck is one of those mysteries for which no answer is to be found. I have never been able to attribute my escape to providential favor, for those who are thus delivered commonly survive to become of some worth in this world.

We had a hound named Whistling Buoy, a great black-and-white beauty that had been secured from the mountains of western North Carolina. He gave me cause to christen him what he was named. The very morning after his arrival I took him on a leash with me into the home woods, walking down some of the old sandy roads just to see whether he would take urgent notice of some of the fresh deer tracks that crossed the old trails. About a mile from the house the hound, which until then had been very intelligent and friendly, suddenly developed a stubborn streak. He pulled back, he whined, he looked at me with the narrowed, glittering eye of a strange misgiving. He appeared badly frightened; he might be sick, I thought. I tried to lead him forward, but vain was my coaxing.

When I stroked his massive head, he threw it back and gave a wildly melancholy howl. It had all the weird eeriness and warning heard in the deep mysterious tone of a whistling buoy. Hence, I christened my minstrel. Again he howled. Then I remembered.

Full five months before this there had been killed, some fifteen feet from where the hound had stopped, a monster diamondback rattler, a veritable chimera. Nearly eight feet it had measured. Its body had for a long time been hung on a little persimmon tree. Nearly a half-year later my new hound caught the dread scent with which the ground had been impregnated, knew what it was, halted on what he knew was the brink of death and warned me to imitate his wariness.

Such incidents as I have described suggest the adventurous nature of my boyhood days, and while some people might have been glad to get away from such an environment, the magic of it all was in my blood: the birds, the animals, the strange reptiles, the lonely mystery of river and wood and swamp. They were a part of my heritage, and to them I longed to return.

One of my chief misgivings about that return came from the fact that I had lost Prince Alston, my faithful comrade. When one has passed the half-century mark and then loses a loving friend who has been most constant and affectionate since boyhood days, especially one on whose support he greatly depended, he hesitates to take up an adventure such as beckoned to me. With Prince's help I should have had no fear of failure; without his aid I knew I would have to enter a fight without sword or shield.

Early in January, 1928, I was leaving Hampton after a

Christmas vacation spent there. Five of us were packed in a little Ford, and we had luggage on both running boards. It seemed to me possible that we might get somewhere, but to get out on arrival was another matter.

Our farewells had been said. I had started the engine. At that moment Prince came to my window, battered cap in hand.

"Cap'n," he said, "can you get out of the car a minute?"

He had helped us get wedged in and he knew what he was asking. But such was my instinctive trust in him that I did not raise any question. Headfirst I clambered out of the window.

Prince led me to one side; then he stopped and faced me.

"Please, Cap'n," he said, "take off your hat. I just want to look into your face once more."

I could not help knowing that he had a deep premonition that we should not see each other again.

August 2, 1928, at Hampton Plantation, there died a man so remarkable that some account of his life should be of interest to all those who take delight in studying character in the great school of humanity. In my estimation, and in the regard of all who knew him, Prince Alston was an original, a vital, a virtuous and a convincing personality. He was a Negro, but of no ordinary sort. He was the kind to redeem not only his own race, but the whole human race as well. For, if essential greatness is to be measured, not by how far a man has come, but how far he has come considering his start, then I never knew another human being to come further than this same humble Prince.

Life offers to some of us a pretty smooth highway on

which to speed along; but for every Negro life is an ob-
stacle race. He starts handicapped; and he is liable to
encounter innumerable obstructions. For the plantation
Negro especially life is a high-hurdle race.

It was Burns, I think, who gently complained that those
who accused him of weakness never realized how much
he had resisted. We who watch the finish of life's regatta
would do well not to turn with scorn from the battered
hulks that come in last. To reach Home they have not
merely sped gaily like gleaming yachts up sheltered water;
in nights of dread and gloom they have rounded the Horn,
weathered the gales off the Falklands, and run the grim
gauntlets of Hatteras. In the great voyage of life Prince
came Home—after spiritually circumnavigating the globe.

He and I were born in the same year on the same estate
and from earliest childhood we were inseparable companions. As I have mentioned, we shared a thousand innocent
adventures in the wild plantation woods, the wide plantation fields, the deep and strange plantation waters. I
developed into an amateur naturalist, Prince into the only
peerless woodsman I have ever known. By the time he was
thirty he was in complete charge of the work of the plantation. Between my father and Prince there was perfect
understanding, trust and that singular and admirable
camaraderie that is one of the most heartening of sights
to human eyes, for it is palpable evidence of that greatness
of heart that effects essential brotherhood.

Certain traits of my plantation comrade stand out clearly,
now that he is gone. One of the most interesting of these
was his almost occult understanding of all creatures, wild

[47]

or tame. The savage bushmen of the forests of the equatorial regions of Africa bring to their pursuit of game a certain aboriginal directness of comprehension that it is beyond the power of the white man to employ naturally, or even to imitate. Prince had this same kind of power, but it was refined. It gained in finesse without losing any of its elementary savor. When I wanted an intractable horse or mule broken, I turned him over to Prince and the miracle was speedily performed. Indeed it was my common experience actually to observe in such a creature a change of attitude and in demeanor the moment this Negro took charge. A hopeless hound under the hand of Prince would become the leader of the pack.

I used to study this magic, but I could never acquire it. There was something in his look, in his gentle, authoritative manner, in his complete and amused comprehension of an inferior, in the level, penetrant voice, that reached the heart of the animal under his care. Absolute obedience and docility followed, and by no other means could it have been effected. I remember how the manager of a great lumber mill sent for Prince, the only man known in that region who could handle an especially vicious four-in-hand of mules hauling an unwieldy timber cart. A few days later I saw Prince riding one of the burly miscreants of his team while he cajoled the other three along in dulcet tones that evidently did not stop short of the place where dwelt their acute sensibilities. They had found a master and they had accepted him contentedly and loyally. I remember a half-wild bull that was the terror of the plantation Negroes, and of others as well. I confess that it was with considerable apprehension that I encountered this shaggy aurochs in the lonely pinelands. The Negroes loved to dilate on the bull's ferocity, and certainly his truculent mien and his massive strength seemed to justify their dread.

"But," they would add with awed pride, "Prince ain't 'fraid of him."

One day I returned to the plantation to find Prince plowing the cotton—with the wild bull!

As it was with domestic creatures, so it was with the dwellers in the dim swamps, the exotic savannas, the solitary copses of myrtle, sparkleberry, and sweet bay: Prince held in his strange but authentic understanding all the secrets of their lives. I learned of wild things partly by observation, but chiefly, I think, through Prince's hints and suggestions. He appeared to regard all beasts and birds as his younger brothers and sisters, and he spoke to them and of them as if he were admitted to all their hopes and fears. There was something very profound in this— something of the true mystic's fathomless far reach to the heart of God. He had a kinship with nature that was as unfeigned as it was intimate. Untroubled, he laid his head on the bosom of the Universal Mother, and he was made peaceful by the quiet songs she sang out of her eternal heart.

It was Prince who would beckon to me to show me a couched deer that I had passed by; it was he who would pause in the still woods to listen with a certain ancient intelligence gleaming in his understanding eyes. Then he would tell me that he heard a wild turkey calling on Buck Ridge, deep in the lonely swamp. He used to talk familiarly of the winds and the clouds, the sunshine and the rain. And he seldom referred to them without in some way associating them with the immanence of God.

Indeed, the faith of this Negro was one trait that I supremely envied. Untouched by any human school of philosophy, he was deeply read in the oracles of God. Aware of the exceedingly brief, almost tremulous, span of mortal existence, he would always make his simple promise contingent upon "if life lasts." A thousand requests I have made of him. Always his answer would be: "All right, Cap'n. I will do it for you—if life lasts." But the brevity of life did not oppress Prince; his faith was too sure. And he died as he lived, in steadfast beautiful loyalty to his belief.

"Now," he said calmly, as he lay dying, "I am going to my heavenly home."

Could Bishop Thomas Ken, or Phillips Brooks, or any other saint of the church have said anything more affecting and reassuring?

As was his faith in God, so was his faith in man, and he made it manifest chiefly in the compassion he showed to his inferiors and the unwearied courtesy he showed to his equals and to his superiors. Infallibly he possessed that priceless treasure that we call good taste. I have been greatly entertained to watch certain bourgeois whites attempt to imitate Prince's quiet manner.

Now that my black Prince is gone, I have lost the right arm of my woodcraft. Because he interpreted nature and her children to me, I cannot ever again have my vision clarified, my heart made aware of wonder, by this humble counselor of mine. But always I can be grateful for all that his unassuming companionship meant to me.

Deep in the fragrant heart of the plantation greenwood there is a sacred inviolate tract, set aside long before the Revolution as a burial ground for the Negroes. A wild sweet place it is, where sleep generations of meek servitors. Here the yellow jasmine riots over pines, azaleas, myrtles and dogwoods. Here the mockingbird pours forth his iridescent song. Here nature seems always to tremble with bridal loveliness. And here, committed to nature's compassionate heart, lies my comrade, who took her joyously for granted, knowing her and loving her as a son his mother.

Chapter 4

The House and Buried Treasure

HAMPTON has always been the mother plantation of this old plantation country. From this house the British Colonel Banastre Tarleton stole the parish Bible and prayer book. Later they were recovered from a book-stall in London. He likewise lifted an ornate volume of a two-volume Baskerville edition of Milton, printed from silver type and bound in scarlet buckram. I still have the second volume, and I hope that some member of the Tarleton family now in England may read these words and return to me the first volume. This home served as the headquarters of General Francis Marion, the daring partisan leader, the renowned Swamp Fox of the Revolution. By the fireplace in the living room stood a Chippendale armchair, wrought of ebony. The left arm, until a few years ago when I had it replaced, reposed in a closet in the room. Once when I asked my father why the arm had never been replaced, he told me that General Marion, after one of his exhausting forays, had been asleep in the chair when the Redcoat, Tarleton, surprised him. In springing up, Marion broke off the arm. He ran through a secret passageway to the back of the house, jumped on his horse tethered there, swam the river and escaped into the great and gloomy wilds of the Santee delta.

"You see, son," my father said, "we always thought it would be sacrilegious to replace what Marion had broken."

During the Revolution, and especially after Charleston had been captured by the British, Hampton became a great place of refuge for friends and relatives from the stricken city. I have letters of that time. In one I read: "There are twenty-six of us here now." When things got too hot in the city, Governor John Rutledge, my great-great-grandfather, journeyed here in what he termed his "chariot." The British failed to capture him, though they took his younger brother Edward, the Signer. When someone asked, after the colonial government had been forced to leave Charleston, "Where is now the capital of the colony?" the reply was, "The carriage of John Rutledge."

In 1791, when Washington made his triumphal tour of the South, he stayed at Hampton. I have many records of that visit. "The ladies," we are told in a family letter of the time, "all wore sashes and bandeaux inscribed with the legend, 'Hail to the Father of our Country.' " Standing on the front steps with a group of ladies, Washington was asked whether a live oak, growing immediately before the house and some sixty feet from it, should be permitted to stand. "Let the tree stand," he said. And it has stood all these years, and has become known as the Washington Oak. The diameter of the space covered by its shade is 115 feet, and yet it is not the largest live oak near the house. There is one with a shade diameter of 142 feet. Four feet from the ground the trunk of this giant is ten feet in diameter.

But it is a letter from Washington to my great-great-

grandmother that affords me a better idea of him than anything I ever read of him in history or in fiction. When
some forty miles away, wishing to apprise his hostess of
the probable time of his arrival, he dispatched a rider
through the night and the rain with a letter. The rider had
to cross the Peedee, the Black, the Sampit and the Santee
Rivers. The letter is a formal affair. It is the postscript that
reveals the real Washington to me. "P. S.," he scrawled
hastily, but urgently, "For God's sake, give my rider some
grog!" As there is a cellar at Hampton—one of seven—
that could have been nothing but a wine cellar, I am sure
that that lonely rider met good cheer on his arrival.

Though there used to be about a hundred acres of
cleared upland, where various crops, including indigo,
were grown, Hampton was always essentially a rice-growing
place. There is one three-hundred-acre field, one of ninety
and several smaller ones. All these are now waste marsh-
land, the haunt of rails, marsh rabbits, blackbirds in dark
myriads, raccoons and wild ducks. Some twelve hundred
acres are timberlands, growing yellow pine; and several
hundred are in swamp, growing black cypress, gum, tupelo
and water oak.

Hampton and its life must have been like many other
plantations and their lives until the Civil War came. That
disaster, however, did not directly touch us. My father was
at the front. The place was left in the care of the Negroes.
Sambo Boykin, a giant slave, carried the mahogany side-
board and the rosewood bookcase to a flatboat, taking them
far down to some hiding place on the delta. When the
danger had passed, he brought them back, and they have

been in place ever since. There is a legend in my family, and I believe it may be true, that the slaves buried a great deal of the family silver, and that it has never been found.

Hampton House, on an eminence above the river, was built in 1730, of brick, black cypress—which is heart cypress—and all-heart yellow pine. In restoring the house I have had occasion to see behind every wall, under every floor, all those places where shoddy work, had it been done, might for centuries have been concealed. But all is massive, true. It seems to be a house affectionately built. The giant sleepers, hewn out with the broadax, are still sound to the core after the lapse of more than two hundred years. I have shown some of the yellow pine studding to architects, and they marvel at its color and its weight. About ten years ago I put a slate roof on the house, and this has done more to preserve it than anything else that has been done. In removing the old roof, we took off seven roofs. It seems that every time the house leaked, a new roof of cypress shingles was put on, right on top of those already there.

Yet, while the timbers and the boards are heroic in their strength, they present one great difficulty to the restorer: many of them are so unevenly hewn with the broadax that, when a smooth wall surface is desired, a great deal of shoring has to be done. But one does not mind this when one has a solid background against which to work. In uncovering secret places, I often come upon relics of the past: an ancient flask, a handmade saw, a spirit-level still good after two centuries, a quaint cup out of which some long-ago workman drank water—if anybody drank water then!

[55]

In 1923, when my father died, Hampton came to me by inheritance. As I was then living in Pennsylvania, the problem of holding the property was serious. Every year I made a few hurried visits; but if anything enabled me to maintain the place, it was the utter faithfulness of Prince Alston's family, who lived in the big kitchen in the yard, looked after the old house as best they could, planted some of the fields and took care of me when I came down from the North. Truly, they preserved the place for me until the time came when I could restore it.

When I returned in 1937 to live, Prince was gone, but his widow and his three sons were there. I arrived in mid-August, hardly expecting to be able to stand the heat, the deer-flies, and the mosquitoes. But the nights were cool and the days not warmer than a far more northern clime. I took quinine every day to ward off malaria, and slept in an upper room. Malarial mosquitoes are rarely active except at night, and they are said not to rise to the second story of a house. At any rate, I kept well through a season when a river plantation is supposed to be deadly for a white man.

I had some plans about restoring the place, but I really did not know where to begin. By rare good fortune I had living right in the yard a Negro named Lewis Colleton, who as a handy man is a kind of genius. He and I spent two days going through the seven cellars beneath the house and the fourteen rooms in it, trying to decide our method of attack. On the first floor are six rooms. I knew that during the first season, if we did these over, we should feel satisfied. Before starting anything I made up my mind that

La Fayette

my fundamental purpose was not to improve, not to elaborate, but strictly to restore. I wanted in every way to preserve the plantation atmosphere. To a visiting architect I lamented the fact that I did not have a million dollars to do this work. His answer has helped me in all I have tried to do since then.

"If you had plenty of money to do a work like this," he said, "you'd probably ruin it."

Lewis and I decided to make a start by papering and painting the six rooms on the first floor, at the same time installing a water system.

Our most ambitious task was the restoration of the ballroom, which occupies the entire east wing of the house. That elaborate, if occasional, entertainments were given on these plantation estates is well attested by the construction of such a room. At the time it was built, one of my forebears had gone to France. There he had married the niece of the Marquis de La Fayette. He sent back from France lovely mirrors to be hung on the huge black cypress panels which are the admiration of architects. They were there until the troublous times of the War between the States. Then the mirrors were taken down and hidden, presumably buried. Their hiding place has never been discovered. The room is forty-two feet long, and the heart yellow pine boards of the floor are all one length. These are said to be the longest floor-boards in America. Imagine what timber grew in those old days! And, of course, all of this was cut right here on the place. The ceiling, which is beautifully arched, is twenty-eight feet high. The arching, I discovered by climbing over the top of it in the attic,

is made by huge cypress bows, in eight pieces pinned together; in fact, a great deal of the house is so pinned. The
side walls of the ballroom are, as I have said, of black
cypress, in one-piece panels. The panel above the fireplace
is seven feet five inches wide. I now have cypress trees on
the place that will yield such boards, but I cannot get them
out of the swamp. In the old days, when such giants were
felled in their humid wilderness, roads used to be cut from
them to the river; then, when a flood swept down the
Santee, they were floated out to the river and thence to
the plantation landing.

How to finish a huge room with cypress paneling gave
me pause. Many of my friends advised that it be finished
in the natural wood. But it had been painted white. I decided therefore to do it over as it had originally been done,
except that I made the ceiling a turquoise blue.

My good Negro Lewis and I hewed down cypress poles
from the near-by riverbank, brought them one by one
through a window in the ballroom, and made our platform
within the room. To scrape this one room and to paint it
took us nearly a month.

The fireplace in the ballroom, more than seven feet
wide, is faced on either side by Delft tiles in color, showing
scenes to suit every taste, from Bacchanalia to Biblical
pictures. For example, there are groups that might have
come from Hogarth; there are lovely nautical scenes; there
are trees and delicate wildflowers; we see David and Go-
liath, the Good Samaritan, nymphs and satyrs, lords and
ladies. Some of these tiles are of a rich deep blue, while
others have white as a background. I had never differen-

tiated them. But one day an Italian artist visited me, and immediately he began to "act up." When his excitement abated somewhat, he told me that the blue tiles were Italian, of the thirteenth century; and anyone who examines them carefully will at once notice an unmistakably medieval air about them. Excessively rare, these tiles are greatly admired.

There is one defect in the ballroom that is not structural: the marble hearth has sprung up from the floor almost an inch. This was caused by the earthquake of 1886, which shook this country considerably. However, I like to think that, although something in Hampton is awry, it took an earthquake to make it so!

During the years before I put a slate roof on the house, leaks were common, and water invariably makes plaster fall. In the dining room, for example, plaster had been falling on my head ever since I was a baby. The plaster on the side walls was bulgy and infirm. Lewis and I tore it off the walls and the ceiling; and as we laid bare the laths, I was interested in their extreme irregularity, for all of them had been hand-hewn; and they were fastened by handmade nails. As soon as we had a level surface on the beams of the ceiling and on the studs, we covered the whole surface with eight by four three-ply boards; on this we put our papering. While it seems rather strange to me now not to have a slab or two of plaster collapsing on my head, I am able to master such nostalgia.

Nearly all furniture is of mahogany, and I believe this was brought in ballast, as logs, from the West Indies. Indeed, it is extraordinary how prodigally mahogany was used. I have a tool rack made of it. One day I was boring a hole through the kitchen floor for a pipe. I noticed the brown sawdust and, to my amazement, discovered that the whole floor is solid mahogany! I suppose that, at the moment, there was a dearth of yellow pine boards, whereas the supply of mahogany was ample.

A great many people have asked me why, in this climate, termites have not undermined the house. The answer is simple: they cannot work on heart yellow pine. It is flinty in hardness. Besides, all the cellars, being almost on a level with the ground, are light and airy, and termites like darkness and dampness. I have been greatly impressed by the fact that the cypress siding on the house, exposed for so many years to rain and sun, has never shown a sign of rot. But it does wear thin. If heart cypress is protected, I believe it will last for a thousand years; indeed, in Italy, there are cypress doors and windows older than that.

These cellars of which I speak must have had a far greater use than they have now. All of them are paved with brick, as is the areaway beneath the front portico. But over these bricks a deposit of silt and sand a foot deep has gathered. Formerly, therefore, the ceilings were comparatively higher—some seven feet from the ground. Two of them have imbedded in their ceilings immense cast-iron hooks, probably for hanging meat. No doubt one cellar was used as a dining room in summer, for the temperature in these rooms is almost constant, winter and summer. Taking advantage of this fact, I made a garage out of the ballroom cellar, and there is never any danger that my car will freeze up.

The walls of these cellars are very massive, of English brick, and but for one great jagged crack made by the earthquake, they appear sound and true after all these years. The most elaborate brickwork is under the front portico, where beautiful cathedral arches support the floor.

As Hampton has always been famous for the abundance of its game, it is natural that there should have been accumulated here a large collection of hunting trophies, especially deer antlers. These used to be in the hallway and in practically every room in the house. As some people did not appreciate them as enthusiastically as I did, I set aside a back room upstairs as a trophy room, and there these relics of the chase are assembled. There are more than three hundred sets of deer horns, and there are scores of other relics from the wilds. One thing that I put there, not knowing where else it might be in place, is a massive silver masonic plaque, a beautiful example of the old silversmith's art. As far as I know, it must have belonged to John Rutledge, my great-great-grandfather, the colonial governor, for he was high in masonic circles. I have in this room the largest deer antlers ever taken in the southeastern United States, and also the record horns of South Carolina for spread between the beams—twenty-six inches.

In this same trophy room is some very wonderful old wallpaper, three layers of it, of ancient beauty and design. The hallway upstairs and several other rooms have other paper as attractive, notably the Blue Room, whose wallpaper has festoons of rose vines and big blue roses. But the most admired is on the side walls of the stairway leading to the attic. This pattern is Olympian in size and Romanesque in spirit. It was made in Ireland about the middle of the eighteenth century. Some of these papers are being reproduced and I hope some day to finish the rooms again just as they once were.

From the first floor to the attic one goes up four flights of a mahogany stairway. It begins to rise from the back of the house, a fact which has puzzled many architects. However, I think the explanation may be that the present back porch, which faces the river, may originally have been the front. Most travel in those old days, especially neighborly travel between the plantations, was by water and most of the plantation houses faced the river. I have an interesting relic that I found here—homemade, and unlike anything else I ever saw. It is a float, a watertight copper box with airtight compartments at its sides. A light was set in this and the quaint contraption was moored at the landing to guide guests by night. It is just one of these little things that remind us that the people of another day lacked nothing in gentleness and consideration for others.

There are eight great pillars that support the roof of the front porch. These are of solid yellow pine, about twenty-four inches in circumference, and tapering slightly toward the tops. In the course of my preliminary investigation of all the woodwork, I discovered that the pillar at the southeast corner had been lowered somewhat by the decay of the wooden base on which it rested, and was leaning outward, unattached at the top. In the next storm I believe it would have fallen.

Lewis and I got guy ropes on it to hold it secure until we

could rig a block and tackle for lowering it; this was done and when we had it safely lying on the front-porch floor, to our amazement, we discovered that the apparently solid pillar had a two-inch auger hole bored in it, throughout its entire length! No doubt the purpose of this was to prevent warping and splitting; but how it was done in that long-ago time is something of a mystery. An architect to whom I mentioned it said that probably the holes were bored through the huge trees first, then they were shaped into pillars, following the lines of the borings.

After making a new cap and a new base for the pillar, we lifted it again into place.

Another architectural curiosity that was uncovered was this: in taking off the side wall of the Red Room, which is the bedroom immediately over the living room, I disclosed the outside of the immense ballroom chimney. Set some two feet away from the side wall of this brick chimney is another brick wall, literally enclosing it, with an airspace between. I suppose that this second wall was to insure fire protection; but the design of it appears unique.

After we had the pillar set back in place, Lewis and I investigated another matter. Between the living room and the ballroom there is a high passageway. On the left is a secret closet, concealed by wallpaper that covers the door as well as the wall. On the right is a similar offset; but this runs clear to the roof, and had never been opened. Moreover, there had always been a strong family tradition that it might contain something—treasure perhaps, or a skeleton!

On this eventful day I went into the ballroom cellar with

Lewis. Much to his misgiving, we sawed through the floor and into the mysterious compartment. When the black chasm of it appeared above us, the heart of Lewis failed him, and he disappeared for the day. I climbed up into it with a flashlight. All was dust and darkness and silence. All I found was a small box and its lightness disappointed me. But inside I found a folded paper. On this was drawn a plan of the house. From one corner a line was drawn at a certain angle, 34 feet 11½ inches. There was even the drawing of a shovel, so that the finder of the map would know what to do. Then there was a cross and the picture of a box. It looked like a treasure chest. But on that exact spot grows a live oak a century old. I have not delved yet for this treasure. But I must. I believe I shall find it.

In another way I have already discovered some of the buried treasure. Putting up a workbench in one of the cellars, I was surprised to find that the floor consisted of a foot or more of solid ashes and sand, out of which I dug an amazing assortment of relics: bushels of broken Wedgwood china, of exquisite design and color (I have managed to put some of these cups and dishes together again); old brass locks and all kinds of intricate homemade fasteners; hinges without number, some of them unique in design; very ancient bottles, magical in their curious shapes and marvelous colors. They are hand-blown, and no doubt the work was done here on the place. I found beautiful brass escutcheons, antique razors, spectacles, implements for hand-loading shotgun shells, keys, frows and some pieces of problematical use.

My best find so far was made in one of the west cellars,

deep in a corner under two feet of ashes. This was a cache of twenty-eight of the beautiful Delft tiles, like those of the fireplace in the ballroom, all perfect and all in color. Some of the scenes on these, as that of the Resurrection, are certainly medieval. Two have upon them lavender wildflowers of surpassing delicacy of color and grace. Since some of them must have been antiques when they were brought to America, no doubt they were hidden away at the time of the building of the house. Some of these tiles are signed by the artists who made them.

The seven cellars not alone held treasure under the ground but above the ground there was a wilderness of junk. From the twelve or more wagonloads of this refuse that I hauled out, there were several things that I kept for my plantation museum: a handmade single-bar harrow; several hand-wrought tools; a huge frow that must have long ago been wielded by some giant Negro slave; a lawn roller made of Italian marble; an old rice fanner; some of the quaintest of the hinges; a mill for grinding corn; a mortar of wood and two pestles, which were used for pounding rice; and a tiny handmade cotton gin, wholly original in design, which antedates Eli Whitney's by a generation or more.

But coming home means more than finding buried treasure. There is a neighborliness about plantation life that keeps it human and refreshing. One afternoon Sue Reeves, whose mother owns the neighboring place of Annandale, drove in to ask me for some little live oaks, saying that she would trade me a camellia japonica for some. I got a dozen for her, and she could have had a hundred for the asking; but the next day, when her truck brought me a five-foot camellia in full bloom, I felt that she had made no bargain. Such a bush would be ten years old, and it was one I could never have bought.

While digging a hole near the house for it on the edge of a sandy field, three feet down my spade grated on something. Carefully I investigated and at length uncovered neatly laid in a perfect row, eleven ancient bottles, brilliant in reds and blues and opalines. They had been deep underground certainly for a hundred and fifty years, and perhaps for much longer. Even their lack of symmetry was attractive, for it bespoke their age and the fact that they were hand-blown.

When they were washed I found fragments of cork and what apparently were wine stains. My guess is that they had been buried full of wine. If they had been merely thrown into a hole as refuse, they would have lain in a jumble and some of them surely would have been broken. But their spacing must have been by design. As I look at them, I wonder what ancestor of mine either forgot where he had his private hoard, or was taken from this mortal scene without ever having had the opportunity of enjoying what he had so artfully hidden away. I might add that in general cleaning up I have discovered more than two thousand antique bottles, jugs and jars. The glass in many of them is massive and opaque; in others it is exceedingly delicate and translucent. Some are canary yellow; some are brilliant green; some are a strange deep blue; but I think the loveliest are lavender—sometimes almost purple. Even ink bottles of a century ago are interesting, while

[66]

elaborate old flasks suggest by their historical and political designs their ages and what people of their day were thinking of. And some day I may run across buried silver, or perhaps a rusty chest full of gold sovereigns of good Queen Anne. My forebears must have buried some of their wealth. They left it to me, but neglected to tell me where they left it.

Finding so many relics and wishing to display them to visitors, I decided to make a plantation museum in the huge old front room of the kitchen, which is an entirely separate building from the house but complementary to it in design. All through my boyhood everything was cooked there and brought in the house on big covered waiters. In this room is a cavernous fireplace, andirons with hangers for spits and Dutch ovens. In this room I have placed on display most of the typically plantation antiques that I have found here. Nor does a day seem to pass without my being able to add to the collection. In the other rooms live Prince Alston, son of the first Prince, and his wife, faithful guardians of Hampton and I am building not far from the old kitchen, a house for Sue Alston, Prince's widowed mother, who is and has always been the guardian angel of the place.

Chapter 5
"Assisting Nature"

WHILE the work in the house was going on, I had small groups of Negroes at other tasks; and I walked many a mile in the September sun to see how each group was getting along. One matter of the greatest help to me was the fact that I could get all the cedar and cypress posts and poles I needed right on the plantation, and usually close to the house. Of course, I had to buy a certain amount of dressed lumber for outbuildings. One group of Negroes built for me a good-sized stable, and wired off an ample stable yard. I am never cramped here for space. The stable yard is a full acre. Three other men erected for me a two-car garage, a smokehouse, a boathouse, a woodshed and an engine house, where I installed a machine for sawing wood and grinding corn. Others built a pump house, where they set an engine for the water system.

But the greatest problem was the underbrushing. Between the house and the woods to the southward I have thirty acres of what had been cleared land. Between the house and the river, to the north, is a yard of some ten acres. On all sides, while I had been away from home, the forest had crept up on me, and to the very doors were weeds, bushes, wild grasses, briars and trees, many of them much higher than my head. Here was a Herculean task, for such growths, if merely cut off, will, in another season, spring up worse than ever. All had to come out by the roots.

As the plantation Negro schoolhouse is only a short distance away, I enlisted the help of the children after school hours, paying them twenty-five cents each an afternoon. About thirty children came. These I segregated into gangs, appointing a boss over each group. And they did a mighty work. Out of a stifling wilderness, out of what the Bible so fitly calls the abomination of desolation, they brought cleanliness, order and beauty. When, therefore, I think of those who have helped to restore Hampton, these children are remembered.

I had warned them—for it was summer—to beware of snakes. Not far from the house they killed four hoary old copperheads and two coral snakes—those brilliant little reptiles which look like ten-cent-store necklaces. They look harmless but, being of the true cobra family, they are deadly. One afternoon I was standing on the front porch watching these children. One of them let out a yell, then was momentarily veiled from view by the dust storm he made in running. I found that he had put his hand on the top of a four-foot live oak to pull it toward him, when he discovered, coiled in the dense top, a big timber rattler.

When Audubon gave to the world his famous picture of a rattler attacking a mockingbird at her nest high off the ground, scientists ridiculed the idea that a rattler can climb. But, though not so skillful as the black snake or the garter snake, a rattlesnake can climb leaning trees or dense bushes or vines where the purchase is good. Once when I was under a live oak, I heard one, but could not locate him. After a time I saw him lying full length amid the ferns growing on top of a massive horizontal limb, eight feet from the ground.

Though a vast amount of underbrushing had to be done, I did some planting also, setting out live oaks, magnolias and wild azaleas. From the woods to the house, a distance of six hundred yards, I planted a holly avenue of 154 trees. Though avenues of other trees are common, I do not know of another of holly. Circling the woods inside the great enclosure and coming up to the house, I planted a walk of native dogwood, eight hundred trees in all. As the great *Magnolia grandiflora* is one of the noblest trees in America, and as young ones spring up in wild shrubberies, I made a nursery row of one hundred of these, hoping some day to find a sale for them. It is not easy at any time to buy a magnolia of the right size and shape.

I transplanted some huge dogwoods by making a sled, then a box which has a tin removable bottom and one detachable side. In that way I can get practically all the earth and roots. And if you wonder how the lifting from its natural bed to the sled is done, and from the sled to the new location, remember the willing and efficient help I have from my Negroes. Because he will always try to do it, I always think twice before asking one of them to do a thing.

I really must tell of the transplanting of one especial dogwood. The incident is too revealing of Negro character. I had found, far back in the wildwoods, where no one would ever see it, a superb tree, thirty feet high, more than a foot in circumference, and loaded with buds. Its massive crown was shaped like an umbrella. Summoning Prince and Lewis, without telling them what was on my mind, I took them to the tree. Then, with no lurking shadow of doubt in my tone as to the possibility of the undertaking, "Boys," I announced, "we are going to plant this tree right by the house."

Never thinking of offering any objection, always tolerant toward my vagaries, they tapped the earth, they eyed the height of the tree in relation to the thicket surrounding it, they paced off the distance to the road. Then, saying only, "We'll be back soon," they melted into the surrounding woods. After a time here came Prince with the sled; Lewis returned, bringing with him Will and Sam. Alex Jones appeared out of the ether with his wild ox. Arthur and Joe and Lisbon came and a half dozen women trooped along to see the fun. Word had gone out that there was something doing, and nobody wanted to miss it.

The tree was dug up with earth and root system intact. A road was cut through the thicket to the main road. The tree was lifted bodily on the sled and tied down with a rope, while seven men supported it. Alex gave all his attention to his ox. This was wise, for this brute had no low or second gear. He could stand or he could run. At his master's ferocious command, this creature broke into a full run, and all the men with it, not to mention the women, screaming and laughing at this strange circus. At the time the tree was scarlet with berries and hung with the tattered gold of autumn leaves. Never can I forget the intermittent but breathless flight that it made down the avenue to the house, where we had a hole prepared to receive it. It was after dark before the feat was accomplished; but the coming of dusk served only to lend an air of festivity to the occasion.

[71]

Invariably the Santee in freshet lays down a rich deposit of silt, which greatly improves land for planting. Frequently this occurs in March. As soon as it recedes, we begin our spring planting. Some people can make money farming. I cannot. I therefore confine my personal efforts to trees, vines, flowering shrubs and plants.

With my Negroes I have a peculiar arrangement about the plantation fields. I help them with the proper seeds and they use my teams for working the crops. They are sharecroppers, but of no ordinary sort. When the crops come in, they give me enough peas, corn, rice and sweet potatoes to run the house during the winter. They take all the rest—probably eighty-five per cent. The benefit I really receive comes from keeping the lands in cultivation. If left idle for a single season, they grow up in pines and broom sedge.

Plantation springtime has a charm about it that owes its magic partly to nature's awakening and partly to man's. It is the time when the fragrant black loam is heaved high behind the plows; when Negroes are torn between a desire to go fishing and a desire to start a crop; when one delightful race of wildflowers follows another, passing from beauty to beauty's bourn. Even the great live oaks bloom, their massive crowns a golden haze. The woods are gaily hung with yellow jasmine and red woodbine. Then the spirea snows her beauty on illumined grass. The Pride of India tree arrays herself in purple, while in dusky watercourses the traveler's joy hangs in lavender stalactites. Out in the lonely woods of pine the atamasco lilies glimmer on the swamp edges; the nightshade hangs her purple lamps; the fringe bushes startle one with their gossamer bridal veils;

and the wild azaleas and dogwoods star the forest with their pink and their snowy blooms.

At Hampton I wanted to bring as much of this native beauty as possible to the plantation house. From the wild-woods I brought the tall wood violets, the white lilies, the dahoon holly (the leaves of which have no spines), the wild azalea, and many other species. Nor was I the only one interested in developing the grounds and gardens. During the past three years generous friends have given me more than five hundred flowering shrubs, trees and vines. Among these are flame azaleas, pink dogwoods, butterfly bushes, camellias, gardenias, iris, amaryllis, wisteria, roses, spider lilies, Daphne and tea olive. My own personal hobbies have been dogwoods and camellia japonicas. The latter I grow from cuttings.

When I began this last venture many friends gave me cuttings; and, more valuable, they gave me advice. I know nothing in horticulture more exciting than to start camel-lias from cuttings and to bring them into bloom. I began by laying off a sheltered space in the backyard, under the live oaks, twenty feet by thirty feet, putting a little fence about it, and burlap stretched against the wire outside to make a windbreak. Then I excavated the top soil to a depth of six inches, filling in then with clean white sand. In the sand I set, flush with the surface, rows of bricks four inches apart. The idea of these is to conserve the moisture of the soil. Stripping the cutting of all leaves but one, and being careful to cut it just where the new growth joins the old, I thrust them into the sand at a slight angle. Whereas formerly it took months to root a cutting, I have found that it can now be done in the same number of weeks by using on the tips the new magic chemical Hormodin. In the manner described I have rooted at and for Hampton more than a thousand camellia japonicas. It may truly be said that the camellia is the queen of the South. One may easily tire of too many azaleas, but never of too many camellias.

Some of my flowering shrubs have been given me by garden clubs which, needing a speaker for a meeting and having no money, offered to pay me in beauty. I can never refuse such an offer.

Since my return to Hampton, all this work of transplanting has naturally brought me to understand certain principles which govern the successful moving of shrubs and it has also taught me something of the individual characteristics and needs of different plants. As the field is wide, I shall limit myself to giving only such hints as may be of immediate interest and helpfulness to the average owner of a garden, a farm and an estate.

There can be no question but certain species are much more readily moved than others; this fact may be due to the nature of the root system, to a difference in native vigor, to causes that we do not yet understand. It is also to be remembered that different members of the same species may have a great difference in natural vitality, just as is the case with human beings. One principle that must be remembered is that a far greater care must be taken with some trees and shrubs than with others. But, up to a certain limit of size and age, all can be successfully moved.

One of the most difficult bushes to transplant is the holly. I have already mentioned that approaching my house

I have an avenue of a hundred and fifty trees. All of them are now bearing berries (of course, I selected female trees, as the males bear no fruit). I began this planting in 1926. It took me eleven years to get this avenue started. I once heard that the holly must be set in its new situation in the same position relative to the points of the compass as it stood in its original place. I believe this to be superstition. My hollies that have died have always been bushes that were taken up with bare roots. Though the roots were kept damp and the bushes watered and mulched with old leaves, all of them died. Even those died from which I clipped all the leaves. In planting evergreens like the holly, the *Magnolia grandiflora* and the sweet bay, I have heard it advised that the bushes (set, of course, in their dormant season) should be defoliated. But I have not found that it made any difference. My hollies that have grown have been medium-sized bushes (from two to four feet high) which were taken up with all their earth and root systems intact.

Another difficult bush to handle, a bush that will eventually develop into a great tree, is the pine—whether it be white, yellow, slash, rosemary or any other variety. However, of these the yellow or longleaf pine is by far the hardest to make grow. The great problem with the hemlock, the pine, the spruce and other similar trees is the great taproot, which should not, in transplanting, be injured. It is almost a miracle if any of these more than four feet high can be moved—at least not without heavy expense. My best success with pines has come from transplanting seedlings, with the entire root system intact. I

[75]

have set 4500 yellow pines in a block and lost only a few; whereas I once set 150 yellow pines that were several years old and lost every one.

In transplanting oaks, a little one can be safely moved if practically all its earth is brought with it. But there is another way to do it and with me this latter method has proved uniformly successful. I have transplanted in this way oaks that were four inches in diameter and fifteen feet tall. I take no account of the earth about their roots; I get out the roots as much intact as possible, then, deciding just where I want the tree to head out, I cut off the entire top. Oaks so planted will look for a while like bare poles; but they will grow out beautifully.

Shrubs or trees that develop long taproots never need the after-attention that bushes do that are lateral feeders. Of this second class are the dogwood and redbud Judas tree. Both have only moderate taproots; but they send out a mass of roots that lie close to the ground. Both are very easy to transplant if certain conditions are observed. These trees really belong in the woods and naturally they rarely grow in the full sunlight. However, if they have to be planted in exposed situations, it is easy to simulate their natural situations by giving them heavy and permanent mulches of leaves. I keep a layer almost a foot deep on my dogwoods in the open; and of these I have more than a thousand blooming and thriving. Of these two fine native flowering shrubs, the Judas grows more readily and grows faster than the dogwood. The white dogwood, by the way, comes true to seed; but the pink or red dogwood must be grafted.

In handling these two shrubs, which grow by thousands wild in my home woods, I always take up the earth with them, held in place by old burlap pinned with nails. I rarely lose one when it is planted in this way. If planted with bare roots, some loss is to be expected. Often, however, these shrubs may stand still for a whole year, their limbs bare but living and green, and the following season they will put out. The same thing is true of the crape myrtle. I always give my dogwoods and redbuds ample peat and old leafmold; these conserve the moisture and give them a wonderful start. I also fertilize them; the three best things to use are hardwood ashes, cottonseed meal and bonemeal. It is astonishing how soon the dogwood can be brought into bloom by a moderate application, in the late winter, of one of these stimulators.

It is commonly taken for granted that all vines, trees and shrubs should be planted during their dormancy. I am not sure of that. I have often planted with scrupulous care dormant stock from a good nursery; and nothing happened. I mean the bushes never woke up. The lovely yellow jasmine can be readily transplanted when it is in full bloom, but not readily at any other time. I go into the woods, cut off a big vine a half-inch in diameter, two feet above the root, pull up the roots, and set the vine where I want it. The next season it will be in profuse bloom. I have also moved hundreds of myrtles, sweet bays, dogwoods and redbuds just as the first leaves are breaking out. They seem, so far as my experience goes, to be more ready to take hold at such a time than when they are in their winter drowsing. As soon as I get one packed firmly into its

[77]

new place, I give it gallons of water, put several bushels of dead leaves about the root, piled up in the shape of a shallow plate to afford drainage toward the central root, and then forget about it. I have transplanted dogwoods that were leafing out and have had them come into bloom. However, in my case, I can get the bushes near my house and they are back in the ground not long after they have been taken from it.

Whenever it is necessary for me to handle stock with bare roots, I have a tub half-full of clay water of the consistency of buttermilk. The roots are kept in this; then, when a plant is lifted out, the roots never really get exposed to the air. It seems a principle of nature that air, especially wind, is fatal to roots. Healthy bushes with bare roots, even if kept to the sun and air for but a few minutes, may be practically dead when planted. Roots belong underground.

Certain plants are most exacting about the soil. The gardenia is very tolerant, is a robust grower, and will thrive in any ordinary garden soil. But the azalea, being a plant of the wildwoods, must have the conditions from which it has sprung. It needs a strongly acid soil. Peat moss and rooted leaves of hardwoods, especially of oaks, and plenty of them, give the acidity that is essential. I have found that pine needles make a good azalea mulch. The wonderful camellia is one of the slowest growing of all flowering shrubs; but it attains great size and age. I know one bush more than thirty feet high and it is a hundred and twenty-five years old. Each year it bears upward of a thousand blossoms. The camellia likes a soil slightly acid; and it loves a mulch of leaves. Bonemeal, cottonseed meal and cow manure may safely be used as fertilizer. I do not know a flowering shrub or tree that will not be more injured than helped by an application of horse manure.

I lose some flowering shrubs such as dogwoods in a peculiar way. When the bucks are in the velvet and ready to rub, they like to hunt for a sapling in a fairly open place. Then they proceed to rub the velvet off their horns and, incidentally, the bark off the young trees! Last season I lost thirty-eight fine dogwoods in this way, nor do bucks stop rubbing when their horns are clean and polished. Far into the mating season, as long as they are feeling pugnacious, they keep sharpening their horns—and killing my trees!

Once I was talking with a Government forester about transplanting. Among other things he said: "If we do anything, it is assisting nature. She is the real worker." I think that expression, "assisting nature," suggests that we should consider always, before attempting to move anything, that nature has produced a living plant; it is supposed to stand in its cradle until that becomes a grave. Along comes brash man to move it. In some ways he is like a surgeon who has a delicate operation to perform; and he must try not to butcher his patient. He must study individual characteristics, and he ought to know the peculiarities of the species. To succeed one needs to exercise great care, gentleness and provision for a happy reception in the new home. Nor, in this swift and changing life, can a human being find a deeper and more innocent pleasure than in seeing the things that he has planted grow into strength and beauty. It can be done, but it takes virtue to do it: the virtue of care, of patience, of intelligence and, if you please, of love.

Chapter 6
Birds of the Delta

ALTHOUGH rice is one of the major crops, not only of America, but of the world, its nature is such that only certain climates are suitable for its planting. Beyond the limits of the regions where it is grown, people know little about its culture. Less, perhaps, do they know of its relation to the great bird kingdom, although this relationship is most important.

During my boyhood at Hampton, and ever since, I have had opportunity to watch the growing of this important grain, and to know the birds that live in or near the rice fields. Here, as at no other place known to me, there are immense gatherings of various species and often huge concourses of different birds, all intent upon feasting upon their favorite food. And here one learns that the best way in the world to attract wild life is to feed it.

Perhaps the commonest and most persistent visitor to the rice fields is the bobolink. Migrating in late August and early September, this bird, known along the Atlantic Coast as the reedbird, but in the South as the ricebird, is, or used to be, a great enemy of the planter. Their autumnal flight brings them to the South when the rice is "in the milk"; that is, while the grains, though formed, are still soft.

At that time of the year the birds are in their yellow plumage; and when they arrive at the rice fields, they are hungry and thin. Within a week, so gorged are they on the rich food on which they feast that they become ridiculously fat; indeed so corpulent that if one falls on hard ground when it is shot, it will burst open.

The migrating flocks are not usually great in numbers, but when these groups gather at a rice field the numbers appear incredible. I have seen the sky literally darkened by them; and when a great flock would rise, the noise they made resembled distant thunder. Over the delta at twilight, when they would settle in the river marshes for the night, the whole sky would be alive with them; indeed, they themselves would seem to be a moving sky.

When I was but ten years of age, I was a regular "bird-minder" of our rice fields. My duty was to scare the birds by firing a gun which had, in place of shot, a flattened buckshot. The whistling of this missile above the birds terrifies them; and I often roused a feeding flock of several thousand birds in this way. The Negro "minders" used to crack long lashes. But still the birds would come. In memory I can see that host gathering.

First, one bird, from a bush on the margin of the river, would venture to alight in the wide golden field. Then perhaps thirty or forty, flying over, would hear his lone call and join him. Then out of the marshes they would come, pouring in from every direction—five hundred, a thousand, five thousand, ten thousand. As they are very sociable, from far-off corners of the field restless flocks would come to join the big parade.

Sometimes I used to creep through the rice in order to get close enough really to frighten the feeding host. This was ticklish work, as I was barefooted and the field had both rattlers and cottonmouth moccasins in it. At last I would come to a few stragglers on the borders of the great host; plump, yellow, bright-eyed birds that I could almost catch with my hand. Then I would hear them feeding: the endless chirring of their bills against the rice grains; the occasional soft note of song; the contented, full-fed note. Now I would be among them. Before me, in an area of rice of not more than half an acre, would be thousands of birds that would rise as a mighty cloud when I fired my flat buckshot over their heads.

On their northward migration in the early spring, the bobolinks reach the rice fields just when the grain is being sowed. At such a time they used to do their greatest damage, for the rice was broadcast on the surface of the wet land, and the visitors, now bright in their gay nuptial plumage, would devour a whole planting. To prevent this destruction, the planters, as soon as the rice was sowed, flowed their fields with water to a depth of several inches. The rice would sprout under the warm water and the vivid green shoots would come up through it. It so happened that I lived through the time when a regular army of Negroes used to be employed to keep the birds off the newly planted rice; and I also saw the time when the practice of flowing the fields began. After a few seasons, finding that the food they love best could not be had, the great hosts no longer stopped in their northward flight. But a few hopeful ones would always come; and as a boy I delighted in seeing the brilliant and jaunty males and in listening to the bubbling of their liquid glee. Because they arrived in May, they were commonly known as May-birds. Few birds, I think, change their plumage so radically; and I could never get the Negroes on the plantation to believe that these gay spring visitors were identical with the yellow hosts of autumn.

Other birds do not greatly disturb rice when it is ripening; but when it is being planted, redwing blackbirds, rusty blackbirds, purple grackles and boat-tailed grackles will not only eat the seed if they have a chance, but will pull up the sprouts. Once, in a far corner of a lonely field that ran into a swamp, I saw a pair of wild turkeys eating the sowed rice.

It is after the rice is gathered that one has the best chance to observe how many birds literally love this grain. They may be considered in two groups—the plunderers and the gleaners. By the plunderers I mean the birds that ravage the tall stalks of rice sheaves. By the gleaners I mean those that search the reaped field for what may be left.

The rice on our plantation used to be stacked in the barnyard between the house and the river. The stacks were eight or ten feet high, and sometimes sixty feet long. Naturally, the topmost sheaves were exposed, and in stacks so large, a great deal of rice was available to the visiting birds. But we rarely molested them. They were cold and hungry and we had plenty of rice.

Imagine on such a stack hundreds of redwings, grackles and rusty blackbirds; scores of cardinals, song sparrows, fox sparrows, whitethroats; now and then a bluejay or two, brown thrashers and towhees. Such a festive gathering could not fail to attract birds that did not eat rice. Thus

I have found amid them many curious visitors: cedar waxwings, mockingbirds, downy woodpeckers, flickers and even great, black, pileated woodpeckers. These, of course, were merely obeying the human instinct to investigate the reason for all the crowd.

While birds are feeding on rice, one hears a continuous shirring sound, as if the sheaves were being moved. This is from the birds' husking the grains. Of all these feasters I ever watched, the cardinal appears most expert at removing the harsh covering of the rice grain, with the redwing blackbird a close second. Nor, besides the noise made in feeding, are the birds otherwise silent. Southern winters are usually mild, and from the tops of the rice stacks and from trees overhanging the barnyard will come cries, calls and occasionally passages of exquisite song. But there are so many voices and they are so varied that their effect is that of a medley rather than a chorus.

Over a period of five years we had on the plantation a wild turkey gobbler that we had raised. I well remember what used to happen when he would fly over the barnyard fence to the top of one of the rice stacks. When once he had planted his great bulk there, he was not content with picking off the grains of rice, but, holding down a sheaf with his feet, he would strip off with his bill the heavy heads of the rice. He made no attempt to hull the grains. When dissatisfied with a sheaf, with his huge feet he would scratch it aside, expose one that was more to his liking. It was to me always spectacular to see this wild gobbler thus feasting alone on top of a rice stack.

Rice is often used as a feed for game birds. Quail are

fond of it. And here we come upon a most interesting sequence of events in nature. Where rice is scattered for quail, rats and mice will gather; and after these, as perhaps his favorite prey, will come the great diamondback rattlesnake. Keepers of quail preserves have told me that they always warn the owners of the preserves not to take their hunting dogs near the places where rice has been scattered, as rattlers are likely to be there. I know from experience that perhaps the most likely place in which to find diamondbacks is in a field of ripe rice. This is because such a place has attracted rats and mice. Several of the largest rattlers I ever saw were killed in a field during the harvest of rice and mice.

There are many birds that are haunters of the rice fields, yet, not being grain-eating, pay no attention to the rice. Thus, at different seasons, it is common to observe there the great blue heron, the night heron, the snowy egret, the wood ibis, the Wilson snipe, the tiny marsh wren, the coot and the beautiful king rail. These dwellers in the marshes love the places and the conditions where rice is grown.

Of the gleaners of the fields, while all species of blackbirds are prominent in these foraging operations, the wild ducks are the most important birds to be considered in relation to rice fields. The true sea ducks apparently never eat rice; nor does the wood duck, as far as I have observed him in rice country. Certainly, if he does, it is with nothing like the relish and the regularity with which mallards, black ducks, teals, widgeons and blackheads consume it. While all these ducks like wild rice, wild celery, tubers of the water lily, acorns, wampee and the acornlike seeds of

[85]

the lotus (and will throng to fields baited with corn and nubbins of sweet potatoes), their favorite food is cultivated rice. In the old rice-growing days in Carolina, when fields of two and three hundred acres were not uncommon, I have seen thousands of these beautiful and valuable wild-fowl thronging in from the ocean and the salt marshes at evening to spend the night feasting in the rice fields. It was a thrilling sight to watch these aerial squadrons deploying above the vast dim fields, and then alighting with happy cries in the shallow waters that glimmered in the rice stubble. As the wild ducks never arrive at their winter home until long after the harvesting of the rice, they are not destructive but are a positive benefit in that they consume many seeds injurious to rice fields, including the rice itself, which, if left, would come up the next season as feeble volunteers.

During the 1937 duck season, I did not have a duck on my Santee River plantation. There were plenty of wood ducks, of course, as there always have been, but I don't count them. I saw lots of ducks flying upward and down the river, saw them by the thousands: mallards, black ducks, teal, widgeons, scaups, and even one stately squadron of about two hundred canvasbacks. What were they looking for? Why didn't they light on my place? A duck looks for water of the right depth, and my plantation didn't have a good duck field. With the passing of rice growing, the banks had been broken by the tides, the field had grown up wild, the water flowed and ebbed at will, and the ducks had left for better places.

Therefore a part of my program of restoration when I

returned to live at my old place was to do something about these ruined fields. It was late in December, after the close of the duck season, that I started to get one in shape. The field, about ninety acres in extent, withdraws from its river frontage far into the mainland woods. The great bank shutting it off from the river is about 150 yards long. For the past thirty years there has been a big break about forty feet wide in the middle of this bank; and through this break the yellow tides dredged, now flowing the field and now emptying it.

Coming through the pinelands on the south there is a little wood stream of clear water that enters that end of the field. I decided to shut off the break and let this stream flow into the field. But the critical thing about the water for fresh-water ducks is to have it at the right depth. My own experience leads me to believe that from eight to fourteen inches is about right. These ducks are not really diving ducks; they just feed "tipping up," and usually they are partly visible while feeding. I once was told by some engineers, who had dammed a great Southern river for hydroelectric and political purposes, that the great lake, ninety feet deep, which had been created, would be an ideal place for wild ducks to feed. They didn't know ducks. Oh, they will light on deep water, they will drowse on it, play on it, kill time on it, but when it comes to feeding, they want the shallows. Any of our fine native ducks, unless fed artificially, would starve to death on water three feet deep.

In order to provide for a constant and suitable depth of water in my field, I cut down about three feet into the old bank, near one end, and put in a spillway four feet wide, using bricks set in concrete on the sides and bottom. Then we got ready to fill the break. In order for a job like this not to cost a fortune, it is necessary not to employ one or two Negroes, but a whole gang; supply them with smokes and coffee, appoint several Negro foremen to create friendly rivalry among the different groups, and then leave the business to them. With eleven Negroes, we spent five days in hauling the clay in wheelbarrows from a near-by bank. Then one afternoon, after our piling had been set, just before dead low water, we began to fill in with the clay we had ready. We had to make sure of getting the fill high enough so that the next tide would not cover it and undo all our labor. I helped with the work until dark, when I went to the house, telling the boys I felt sure we had the fill well above high-water mark. There was a full moon that night and tide was high at ten o'clock. Thinking I might take another look at the bank, I walked across the fields to the duck lake, nearly a mile from the house. As I drew near, I saw a fire on the bank; then I heard laughing and singing. When I got there, the Negroes were still at work; and they had the fill three feet above the brimming tide. In a few days, after we had leveled off the long bank, we planted birches and alders on it to hold it tight.

I ought to mention another advantage of the spillway: it not only keeps the water in the field at proper depth, but in case of a flood (and I have known the Santee to rise thirty-six feet), the first water will pass through the spillway, flow over the field, and thus even the pressure on both sides of the bank.

Having finished that work, I next took up the matter of my water supply. The stream in question was a very modest affair; where it flowed across the road and into the field, the water hardly ran any faster than whisky out of a swamp still, and not nearly so fast as it runs down the throat of a swamp distiller. Taking a gang of my black boys with me, I opened up the stream for about a mile, straightening its windings and taking out logs, brush and leaves. I should say the flow increased fourfold. If any man thinks that his place is impossible for wild ducks on account of a lack of water supply, he ought to examine all the possibilities. The flow from one small spring will fill an immense lake. At first the rise seems to be very slow, as the land drinks up the water and the water has to spread; but when the proper depth has been attained, the height is likely to remain constant, even in a dry time.

After my dam, spillway and water supply had been taken care of, I had nothing more to do but wait to see if any ducks would discover my lake. As I have said, the wood ducks were already there; indeed, for a generation they have nested in hollows on the fringes of that old field. Although we had little rainfall, the lake began to fill up and to back up far into the woods. To it came all kinds of aquatic birds. I saw a few ducks looking it over, but I did not realize what was happening until, exactly two weeks after the break in the bank had been closed off, my cook, Sue Alston, went to a heavy camp meeting one night. The next morning she was very late to breakfast, and when she appeared, I knew that something had upset her soul. Something had scared her.

After some questioning I discovered that she had returned from church after midnight by way of the bank at the duck lake. It was very dark. She was alone, probably deep in religious thoughts. Suddenly, she said, a black cloud full of thunder (and lightning, too, she claimed) rose up out of the field, filling the air with smoke and brimstone and fire. She heard a noise like an earthquake (she had been in the earthquake of 1886). She was so scared that she ran two miles back into the woods, and then came home by the graveyard—a thing a Negro is usually too scared to do. Not a word here is exaggeration, and I was somewhat disturbed myself to account for Sue's fright. I therefore called her son Prince into consultation. As he listened, a slow smile broke over his dusky countenance.

"Ain't nothin' but de duck," he said.

"What?" I asked.

"All de duck in de world," Prince assured me. "I come home las' night too," he added (though it hadn't been from church), "and I hear them and see them. I say, 'This can't be on Hampton.' "

"When did they come in?" I asked.

"They begin to take the field yesterday, comin' in about four o'clock. I done hear them go out this mornin' 'bout daylight. It sounded like a war or a weddin' or sumpin'."

It was with great impatience and curiosity that I waited for the afternoon to come. Two things surprised me about Prince's report: the promptness with which the visitors arrived and the numbers in which they came. I had not seen them as yet, but Sue's genuine fright and her son's explanation of it were sufficient for me.

Before I tell you of what I did see that afternoon, I want to say that it has long been my conviction that flying birds (at least those that make flights of considerable length every day) steer their course by natural objects on the landscape beneath them. The Indians of Canada maintain that the Milky Way points due north and south during the vernal and the autumnal migrations; and that the wildfowl set their course by it. I don't know if they do or not, but I would not put it past them. When I was a boy, we used to shoot wood ducks in a vast old rice field of some four hundred acres. The field was then in cultivation, and the banks were all cleared of trees and bushes. But right in the center of that vast level area, at the intersection of the two master banks, there was a gnarled old cypress—the only tree in the entire field. Well, if anyone wanted to kill ducks, he stood under that tree. They would surely come over it, regardless of the direction from which they entered the field. Later observations have confirmed my opinion that wildfowl set their courses by certain natural objects such as streams, hills, trees and perhaps houses. During a residence of more than thirty years in Pennsylvania, I observed only one bald eagle flying over a valley; but in the autumnal migration I have counted as many as twenty of these great birds flying low over the crests of the Tuscarora Range, following that course from the Susquehanna to the Potomac.

About an hour before sundown Prince and I repaired to the duck lake to see what we could see. As the season was closed, there was no question of shooting. By the time we got there, there were ducks in the field: plenty of wood ducks, a few teal, some widgeons and the scaups or blackheads coming in. I stood where I could watch the direction of their coming. They seemed to follow the river until just before they reached my plantation house; then they flared over the pines and oaks to the east and came directly over the great white home standing on the riverbank. Nearly all these ducks were scaups, but there were some mallards and a good many black ducks. From the house they headed over the wide cornfield until they came almost to the lake. At that point of entry it is flanked by some tall pines and cypresses. All these visitors, coming now in flocks of from five to fifty, executed the same maneuver: they towered suddenly to avoid the trees, and then came down into the field on roaring wings. I have seen great concentrations of wild ducks in many places, both recently and a half century ago. I don't believe I ever saw anything more exciting than this. These birds weren't coming to look the place over; they were coming to light. Before the sun was down, there were thousands in the field; and as the sun disappeared and twilight gathered, the ducks came in much larger flocks. I estimated some of these flocks to number at least two hundred. The place was alive with them.

Prince and I got in a canoe and paddled up the big canal through the field. Many of the ducks rose, but they went only a little way. I did not see one leave the field. When dusk settled down, they were still coming in; and with the stillness that falls over the world at such a time, we could hear them feeding. In fact, when I got back to the house, I could still hear the myriads in the marsh and the duck-oats, the wampee and the smartweed, the lotus and the water lilies.

Every afternoon they came; every morning just before sunrise they left. I would see the whole western sky black with them. This kept up in a routine way until March 16. That afternoon when I went down to the lake, the ducks, instead of coming in, were going out. They had spent the day in the field—a thing they had never done before. Prince was troubled with superstitious thoughts.

"It's nothing," I reassured him. "I don't think they'll be back tonight. They have changed their routine because they are going to migrate."

My conjecture was right. Meanwhile many other wild things have found the lake a convenient home. Bass are in it, and bream; some snowy egrets spent the spring and summer there; a family of little alligators has moved in.

My experience has taught me that wild ducks are not hard to get. With so many crazy things being done to drain their natural marshes and to dam up their natural streams, they are now in search of suitable waters and feeding grounds. Regarded by many of my friends as a barbarian because I hunt, I still feel no guilt in killing wild creatures in a sportsmanlike manner, and when I get too old to get a gun to my face, I'll still just have to watch wild game or lie down and die.

Chapter 7

More Birds of Hampton

BECAUSE of the increasing interest in birds all over America, and because I am most fortunately located for observing them, it should be worth while to record the birds I have observed here on this ancient plantation. Some five hundred acres of my place are in waste rice lands, which are a natural sanctuary for many aquatic species. Two hundred acres are of cleared upland, under cultivation. About twelve hundred acres are in wildwoods. On the place are eighteen natural ponds or lagoons; I have told of making one artificial lake. The marshes, the forest, the fields, the abundant water—all these attract an unusual number and variety of birds.

It is a habit of my life always to be out of the house before daybreak. There are sights and sounds, there is a glory on the world then that it hardly wears at any other time. And I treasure the memories of things seen and heard then.

At daybreak one November day, in the golden heart of a pine forest magic with autumnal colors and fragrances, I was waiting for the possible sight of a wild turkey that a friend had declared he would drive my way as he rode toward me through the woods. What I expected to see was a tall, snakelike neck and a bronzed, broad back came sedulously, glisteningly and silently forward through the broom sedge and the huckleberry bushes. Instead of that I saw a vain but thrilling race—indeed, as extraordinary an affair as a man ever witnesses.

My friend, riding a swift and sure-footed marsh pony, came out of a thicket of young pines about four hundred yards directly in front of me. Between us lay a level stretch of forest, with a few big pines here and there and a soft growth of tawny broom grass on the wildwood floor. Just as he cleared the thicket, the horseman rode up a wild gobbler, which probably had heard him coming for some time and had squatted under some brush. From this shelter he had finally been roused.

What first attracted my attention to the picturesque performance now beginning was the sudden violent start that the horse made in my direction: he came at a wild, driven gallop. Then I saw the great bird above him, superbly beating his way toward me. At the start of this remarkable race the gobbler was thirty feet above the horse and about as many yards ahead. Clearly my friend's game was to try to beat the wild turkey to me and incidentally, perhaps, to prove his pony's speed, about which he had been amiably regaling me with some tall tales.

On came this singular and harmless hurricane. And most thrilling it was to watch. The pony having fully entered into the spirit of the adventure, and the wild gobbler being aware of some sort of strange menace to be escaped only by the most rigorous valor of flight, there was a real race between the two.

The flight of a wild turkey is always impressive, but peculiarly so when, having gathered momentum by beating his powerful wings, he sets his pinions and sails at cyclone

[95]

speed—head far extended, feet far extended—swift without exerted motion, onrushing silently, a living airplane, sentient, electric.

The length of time that a wild turkey can sail seems to depend chiefly on the original height obtained. Many observations of the flight of this magnificent *voyageur* of the sky confirm my opinion that a wild turkey, upon taking wing, usually attempts to attain height first of all; then he gives attention to the details of direction and speed.

Because my friend and his pony had been close upon him ere he took wing, this gobbler I was watching was not able, evidently, to waste time in mounting, thinking it discreet immediately to put all the direct distance he could between himself and his pursuer. The turkey therefore was never more than forty feet from the ground.

With the luxurious autumn sunlight glinting iridescently on his bronze feathers, with the tall yellow pines, and the blue sky, and the glimmering, far swamp of treebays and loblollies and sweet myrtles making a perfect and appealing background for the approach of winged majesty, on came the illustrious fugitive, while beneath him, but every moment falling behind, thundered the excited pony. Above me now the great bird gleamed, splendid and swift, gliding high among the clean pine boles on level, dark wings. He passed, the light on him brightening, fading, flaring softly again. Far through the joyous forest my eye followed him until he was lost in the quiet, mysterious merging of faint sky and golden leaves and that retired, distant loveliness where beats the forest's heart.

A few seconds after the gobbler had disappeared, my

friend arrived on his breathless mount. In the race of about a quarter of a mile the turkey had gained, as nearly as I could estimate, about a hundred yards; but his gaining was continuous, so that there was no doubt of the fact that the pony was outclassed. The matter can be reduced to simplicity when we say that a wild turkey can easily fly on the level at sixty miles an hour, which is a speed no horse can maintain—or perhaps even attain. In flights downhill a wild turkey achieves an almost incredible velocity; and though, as a bird, he makes comparatively small use of his wings, when he does perform, the spectacle is memorable. He always makes me think of a modest champion—unwilling to make a show of himself, but superb when once in action. As a means of escape a wild turkey depends on his legs rather more than his wings. In this respect he resembles the Mongolian pheasant, which runs great distances before dogs and pursuers.

The eagle is also superb in flight and, though not so impressive, many of the hawks are as beautiful on the wing as our national bird. Of the hawk family, remarkable for the grace and speed of their flight, the broad-winged hawk soars highest; indeed, I have watched him when he so towered as to be almost lost to sight, a startling, faint speck in the "blue tracts above the thunder."

Tennyson speaks of the eagle as living close to the sun; and William Vaughn Moody as being a "swift familiar of the sun." But, illustrious as he is, the eagle does not habitually attain the altitude of the broad-winged hawk. I have often wondered why this particular bird chooses to wheel so high above the earth, far beyond any prey that he can possibly hope to catch, or even discern. The one reasonable explanation is that a living creature, merely because it does not happen to be man, is not therefore precluded from that natural joy which Byron meant when he wrote:

> There is a pleasure in the pathless woods,
> There is a rapture on the lonely shore.

Although no man can speak with certainty of the exact relative speeds of members of the same species or of different species, the swiftness of whose flight cannot with preciseness be gauged, yet to all appearance the duck hawk, which is the illustrious peregrine falcon of falconry, a sport with a rich background of history and of picturesque legend, is the fiercest, the most daring, and the speediest of all birds of prey. Its swiftness needs no further emphasis of confirmation than the fact that this lordly pirate of the air captures the ruffled grouse on the wing—a surpassing feat. Walt Whitman would apparently award the palm to the man-o'-war bird, of which he declares,

> At dusk thou lookest on Senegal;
> At morn, America.

But he was speaking most poetically.

One day in the lonely marshes of Tranquillity, in the Santee delta, I was witness to a spectacular contest in speed between a Wilson snipe and a duck hawk. For the game bird this race was, of course, a matter of life and death; and whenever this is the case, any living thing so jeopardized appears to draw on deep reservoirs of energy which ordinarily lie untapped.

I was standing on an old bank with a wild sea of marsh

rolling westward in golden waves. It was mid-October, and I was out in the wasteland country to watch the newly arrived autumn migrants: many shore birds there were, and wild ducks, night herons, a few woodcock and many Wilson snipe. It just happened that I had my eye on this last bird, nervously darting toward a tuft of watery sedge, crouching, and then stealing with artful furtiveness to another tuft when, out of the wide-winged sunset, like some beautiful avenging phantom, a peregrine falcon suddenly appeared. The snipe must have perceived that he was the intended victim, and he must have judged that his best, perhaps his only, chance of escape was in flight. With startled, sharp cries he sprang from the morass and was away on his dashing, dodging, enigmatic flight. The breathless pursuit of this fine game bird by the duck hawk I had an excellent chance to watch, for the sky above the marshes was still radiant with an effulgent afterglow.

I took it for granted that the superb peregrine falcon would overtake the frantically darting fugitive, which had not at best a start of more than a hundred feet, and that distance the hawk could cover in a single second. But what the falcon had in celerity the snipe matched in craft. To begin with, the game bird, much to my surprise, instead of dashing off low over the marshes, suddenly towered, as if safety lay in the zenith. The hawk, a veritable corsair of the sky, of course followed, with a velocity so great that, on account of his swerving at high speed, my eye frequently lost him. That he gained on the English snipe is certain, for again and again he struck at his prey; but in the fraction of a second that it took him to deliver his stroke, his quarry had left the appointed place. Moreover the pursuer lost distance every time he rose above his prey and lunged for it.

Clearly in the pearly twilight I could watch this dramatic race, and I saw the end of it. The proud peregrine falcon, after having attempted desperately to achieve his design, suddenly broke off in disgust, disdainfully, like an aristocrat who withdraws from a contest in which he discovers a menial winning. The snipe escaped in the kindly vastness of the glimmering sky, and the duck hawk haughtily beat his way off toward a lodging for the night in the looming pines at the terminal of the huge delta. Despite the fact that the falcon failed to capture this game bird, I believe that when he is really in earnest, the duck hawk is as swift as any other bird.

One of the most common summer residents at Hampton is the chimney swift. Scores of them nest in the cavernous old chimneys. Not so much for swiftness, but for tireless energy on the wing the chimney swift is extraordinary. As with most swallows, having no purpose to walk, this bird has negligible legs and hardly any feet. But his wings compensate. For the size of his body, his wings are prodigious in length, and of a grace and contour to which the makes of airplanes might well give heed.

Unlike most birds, this independent elf for at least two months after the spring migration gives no thought whatever to the matter of nesting. He spends all these weeks ecstatically on the wing, now flying low in heavy weather, and now high on bright days. At last, when he condescends to build, he snaps in flight dead twigs for his nestlings' cradle.

Thos. Lynch, Jr.

One day a Negro came to me to report that he had seen two old wild turkey gobblers in a sandy field near the river. As usual, word of wild game stirred me to action, and I at once accompanied him to the place. It was the field that once belonged to the plantation of Thomas Lynch, Jr.

With the Negro I crawled up to the edge of the thicket and peered through the rotting fence toward the river. Not more than sixty yards away I saw a wild gobbler standing— a superbly wary creature. The perfect picture of alertness, his head held high, all his feathers drawn in trimly, he stood apparently alone.

"I thought you said there were two," I whispered to my guide lying beside me. But my companion had seen truly.

"Cap'n," he answered, "look on the ground."

This I did; and almost under the first bird, that was standing so erect and sentry-like, there was another, literally wallowing in the warm dry sand of the cotton field. He was wholly relaxed, all fluffed out, and was thoroughly enjoying himself, while over him his old wildwood pal kept watch. After a while the gobbler on the ground arose, shook himself prodigiously, so that the air surrounding him was filled with dust and tiny feathers, preened himself a little, and then suddenly became alert as his fellow relaxed and lay down in the dust bath. They were too smart to wash together; first one took up his post as sentry, then the other.

This incident illustrates a principle common in wild life, that of posting watchmen. We have our policemen, our soldiers, our highway patrolmen, our guardians of the public safety. In some such way both birds and animals often station their sentries; and this is especially true when some members of a group are feeding or are otherwise off their guard.

There are not many birds that do not have some regular system of watching and then of signaling when danger is feared. But I think the mockingbird is the only bird I know that, taking up its residence in a tree, will watch for all intruders (including man), and will attempt to drive them fiercely away. With many birds, of course, a like performance takes place during the nesting season, and the kingbird is inclined to be especially touchy about trespassers. Hence had he his Latin name, *Tyrannus tyrannus,* the tyrant of tyrants. Who has not seen him fiercely pursue and put to ignominious rout other birds, however large, that approached his nesting tree? But the mockingbird is inclined to inhabit a certain tree throughout the year. It is his castle, and he guards it well. According to my observation he loves a red cedar, or a tree smothered in some evergreen vine such as smilax or climbing honeysuckle. He is his own sentinel, ever watchful, and not kindly disposed toward visitors. I sometimes think that birds of high artistic temperament such as his are far more sensitive toward intruders than are commoners.

One day I was crawling down through a ditch that crosses my cornfield in order to shoot into a flock of crows that had been playing havoc in my corn, pulling up the young stalks in order to get the sprouted kernels. On top of a dead cherry tree on the ditch bank there was an old sentinel crow, whose sole business was to keep watch while his fellows ate up my corn at their ease. For some reason he did not see my approach, and I got near enough to the flock to shoot into them and give them a great scare. As they rose, I noticed that they set up an unusual cawing; and as the drowsy sentinel who had betrayed his trust joined them, I saw that they were cawing at him. Moreover, they struck at him angrily. They seemed really more interested in punishing him than in escaping from me. As far as I could see them and hear them, until they disappeared over the tall yellow pines, they kept berating their disgraced comrade and beating him. It is not alone in human life that betrayal of a trust is justly regarded as among the worst of crimes.

A great many stories are told of the so-called "charming" of birds by reptiles, especially by the rattlesnake. This performance I have witnessed many times. But there seems nothing especially strange or occult in it. The dread presence of a rattler has the same terrifying effect on small animals as well as birds; and for that matter, on large animals as well. I have had more than one good horse literally go wild in the woods when he detected the odor of a diamondback.

The fluttering of a bird and its cries of distress upon finding itself close to a serpent are often due to the fact that it is attempting in a pitiful way to defend its nest or its young. At other times the bird may be simply hysterical with fear. I have seen human beings, under similar circumstances, behave in almost that identical fashion. It seems to be a matter of being violently disconcerted, or almost scared to death, rather than being "charmed."

A singular performance is that of turkeys, wild or tame,

when they come upon a snake. Once, in the early autumn, in the open pinelands of the South I was privileged to see a flock of twenty-one wild turkeys discover a rattlesnake. The snake lay on an open arena of white sand, and about him the great birds formed a perfect circle and kept moving in that circle around and around the puzzled reptile. All the while they kept up a querulous calling, half-frightened, half-threatening. I observed that they neither walked nor ran, but appeared to be performing some kind of dance such as we associate with rituals. From my place of hiding in the baybushes, I watched this strange spectacle for nearly half an hour. The turkeys never ventured near the rattler, and the rattler never left his coil. The dry song of his bells rose and fell with the increase and the diminishing of the birds' dancing and the intensity of their cries. At last the flock trooped away into the shadows of the wilderness, still complaining in treble tones of this intruder into their earthly paradise.

Migration is a phenomenon too great and thrilling to be taken as a mere matter of course. When northward through the night goes a clanging chorus of wild geese; when one hears wings and far cries from the upper darkness haunting the purple deeps; when one senses that this is the triumphant van of the irresistible armies of the spring; is not the heart, by these lone and daring trumpeters, summoned to rejoice?

It is during migration that the telephone of the wild is most active. By it lines of communication are kept intact. It makes the hosts cohere. There are continual cries of guidance, reassurance, and of being reassured. The wild geese are going to Athabaska, perhaps; and all of them are talking about it. The mallards are headed for Hudson Bay; they know the route, but they keep encouraging one another mile after mile. If there is a straggler, they pick him up by radio. The vast and solitary darkness is atingle with vivid and vital communications of these children of nature.

This region is an anteroom of spring. It is a vernal vestibule. Here, while the vast expanse of country to the northward is still blizzard-bound, while the snow lies deep, and the icy, unrelenting wind grieves through bare boughs and over frozen ground, spring pauses in her journey up the land as if she would array herself for a bridal. And the joyous companions of spring, her heralds and her minstrels, the migrating birds, here rest from their epic flights in order to don their nuptial plumage, to sing their sweetest songs, and even to select mates for themselves, though their summer homes lie many a league away.

From afar these singers have gathered: from the pampas of the Argentine, from the dim and humid forests of the Amazon, from aromatic isles asleep beyond Florida and the Gulf of Mexico. But, however remote and however alluring may have been their winter Riviera, the Voice has infallibly and importunately reached them. And there has been universal response; for it is to the heart of life itself that the voice of love is calling.

Another consideration that impresses the beholder of this annual wonder is the certainty and the punctuality with which even the least voyagers arrive. Through the immensity of the night, over trackless wastes the gossamer wings of the ruby-throated hummingbird bear him as safely to his far desired haven as do the mighty pinions of the great wood ibis; the grebe on his pitifully frail wings arrives as surely as does that graceful living airplane, the swallow-tailed kite. The delicate cerulean warbler is on schedule time together with the whistling swan and the wide-winged egret.

Northward are they hastening, but they pause for a few days in the region of my home, filling the lonely woods and the solitary marshes with ecstatic song.

In Carolina the great bald eagle is the first of all the birds to mate. The nesting of this king of the air may begin as early as November; and by Christmas I have found the young in the aerie. The horned owl or eagle owl is second, and I have observed fledglings in the nest (always in a hollow and usually in primeval woods) in February. The wild turkey hears the call of spring early; for I have heard the clamorous love challenges of the gobblers begin the first of March. While Flora, in the country to the north of us, is still a wintry maiden sitting as if to have her picture taken with a snowy cape over her arm, the shy woodcock is nesting in my home woods.

I remember observing with a little too much interest a woodcock nest, from its inception until the young were hatched. Finally the gentle and apprehensive mother decided to seek a new home. While I watched fascinated from a sheltering screen of some smilax vines, she nuzzled her little elfin brood with her long bill, finally selecting one for transporting. With this downy baby between her legs she rose on fleet wings that threaded with swift enigmatic precision the blossomy thickets, and vanished into the wilderness of the wildwood. In such a manner she carried each of her babies away.

One feature of the pre-nuptial festival that commands special interest is the fact that, while all these birds are actuated by the same ancient instinct, some migrate farther to fulfill their shining dreams than others. And what makes the marvel of still more wonder is that some have been with us all winter, while others have come prodigious distances.

Nor is the selection of the place of mating determined by the species only. Most members of the woodcock family find their summer homes far north of the Mason-Dixon Line. While the mallards and black ducks and widgeons make a heroic flight to their nesting grounds amid the Athabaskan sedges, I have found them mating at home. But there is a pathos about their staying, for those that linger have been too severely wounded by hunters to join their comrades in the migration. They seek out among their fellows, mates who have been similarly handicapped. All the robins leave us; but some of the kingbirds stay, and some of the redwings, the vireos and the other warblers. Most of the lovely wood ducks spend their mating days with us, yet some travel six or seven hundred miles before they find nesting localities.

Most gentle and most beautiful of all American wildfowl is the wood duck, which seems invariably to nest in a tree. Sometimes the nest is placed in the strong forks formed by larger limbs leaving the trunk; sometimes it is in a hollow—and in this case the wood duck has often been known to use the deserted nesting and sleeping hole of the black pileated woodpecker, and even of the great horned owl! Almost always the nest is near the water, often over the water itself; but occasionally a nest will be found a mile or more away from the nearest pond or river. I know of one nest on the North Carolina coast which is built in a hole in a holly tree in a man's yard! This shows that the wood duck is not afraid of man when it can sense that man will not harm it. This, indeed, is true of practically every wild thing.

Coming one spring day to an old wire fence that sagged its way into the lagoon, I heard a slight noise before me in a small group of cypresses. I thought that gray squirrels were playing in the trees, for they are very fond of eating the tender leaves of the cypress and of romping in these sheltered retreats. A second sound, however, told me that I had come upon a family of wood ducks. One of the cypresses was much larger than its fellows; and it was in a low fork of this, as I now observed, that the mother duck had her nest.

The nest itself was a slight affair set tightly in the crotch and deeply lined with down from the breast of the female. I saw the mother on one of the adjacent limbs. She was talking in a curious way to her babies, which I could barely distinguish as a dark group in the nest itself. The male duck I did not see.

Suddenly the mother—how beautiful and gentle were her movements!—stooped over the nest, picked up one of the young in her bill, lifted it carefully, held it clear of the limb and over the water just a few feet below—selecting, I could tell, a safe place on which her baby could fall—

and then dropped it. The little black ball shot downward, landed with an elfin splash in the water, immediately righted itself, and began to paddle about gayly and happily.

In this precise manner the mother deftly and warily dropped from the nest the entire brood. The little ones were about the size of baby chicks and, as I have said, were black. When the brood of nine was on the water, with a delicious note of relief and contentment the mother herself settled there; and then I became aware of the gorgeous male duck, which must have been near all the time. He came swimming out of a patch of marsh and wampee, joined his family, and they moved quietly and gracefully off into the lagoon.

I recall seeing one day a great flock of bluebirds, hundreds upon hundreds, flying joyously through these airy woods, warbling sunnily all the while like aerial rivulets. It is memorable to see two hundred of these cerulean-clad visitors sweep downward to the dry crests of fallen pines, fairly drifting to the woodland floor.

Of all the troubadours that rejoice in heralding the springtime, none is to me more fascinating than the Baltimore oriole. When he sings from a tall green bough of a live oak, his hearty melody floats like a bright blue banner, luring hearts to follow that flag to a land of dreams. Like a blown blossom or a gorgeous autumn leaf he flits from bough to bough, regal in his tawny-and-black bridegroom's dress. On their northward journey the males arrive first, and they depart before the females come. All day these gay-coated cavaliers carol and call, brilliant firebrands burning against the deep emerald of the leafing trees.

To me the bright wonder of the young year arrives with these birds, and I hear in their singing the calm certainty of joy's return. All that wanders and is wild and beautiful in them finds a voice; they are the meaning of the loveliness that glimmers in forest graces.

Chapter 8
It's a Dark Business

FROM what I have said so far about my Negroes here at Hampton, you might suppose that they are perfect. But even here in these primeval wilds the labor problem crops up, though not in ordinary ways. I have to deal with it every day but my troubles are diffcrent, as you shall see.

Every employer of labor anywhere certainly has his hard times; and in the industrial world these problems are often much the same in character. But with me, and with every employer of labor in the far South, the situations that arise demand more attention to the vagaries of racial character, to the peculiarities of human temperament than any other kind of employment known to me. Considering the people with whom I constantly have to deal, and with whom thousands of other plantation owners have to deal, their employment is almost wholly a psychological rather than an economic one. For example, I can never forecast how many Negroes are coming to work for me, when they will arrive, or when they will decide to "cease firing," as it were. A genuine Negro always feels that work is a kind of imposition, obtruding itself on the joy of life; it is always secondary to the grand primary business of getting happiness out of life. He is an oriental. I do not consider his philosophy inferior to ours; it is just different. As a matter of fact, we labor that we may enjoy. The Negro knows the high art

[111]

of getting joy out of life itself, while we (often vainly) try to get joy out of the money we make by spending our lives in toil. When I say the Negro, I mean the one I know best —the black man of the hinterlands of the Deep South, of the farms, the lonely seashores, the plantations, the wild-woods.

The first difficulty that I, as an employer, have to face, is that the Negro has no sense of time. There are about seventy-five of my dusky friends living either on or very near Hampton. They are the descendants of the old slaves of the place, and if they ever heard of Emancipation, that word certainly did not inspire them to move away from home. They have their humble homes, their church, their school. They keep up fairly well with the passage of the seasons, naming them according to their several delights: Blackberry Time, Watermelon Time, Lay-By-Crop Time, First-Frost Time, Hog-Killing Time. But he is usually uncertain of the months, dubious of the identity of the days, and naïvely unconcerned about the hours. Profoundly respectful toward the weather, which he takes as coming straight from the hand of God, he never criticizes it; and neither for love nor money need you expect a Negro to appear for work on a frosty morning. Once when I protested against this 11 o'clock appearing, I was told, "God ain't never meant us to fight frost." However, in fairness let it be said that while cold gets the Negro, heat never does. Glisteningly he labors in a sun that would slay a white man.

To illustrate better what I mean by a Negro's lack of a sense of time, I may say that I have a standing offer with them of a bonus of ten cents for anyone who will bring me immediate word of any wild game that he has seen. And let it be remembered that a Negro invariably sees more wild creatures than a white man. The Negro's quiet way of walking, his lack of stealth and of purposeful intent, his happy blending with the plantation landscape—these things and perhaps others beyond my ken enable him to see much wild game that would be frightened by a plantation owner.

One day Isaiah came hurrying to me breathlessly to report that he had seen a flock of nine wild turkeys—all gobblers. He told me the exact spot where he had seen them, said that he had not frightened them, and gave the direction in which they had been feeding. I was about to get my gun and shells; I had already paid my dusky informer, when a sad thought assailed me.

"By the way," I asked, "*when* did you see these turkeys?"

Isaiah thoughtfully calculated.

"Well, sah," he said, "it would be about last Friday a week ago."

A plantation Negro's inability to count is also one of those things.

"Flora," I will ask, "how many days have you worked this week?"

Smiling as if caught in her weakness as a mathematician, she will say,

"Well, sah, either two or six."

The latitude here allowed calls for some show of character in my estimate of what I owe her. But in this task I have a masterly aid in my Negro foreman, Prince, who can, without being able to read or write, tell me each worker's "time." He has some mysterious system of his own, and I have never heard a complaint made against his figures.

Flora is one of my few Negro workers who is regularly employed. She works on an average of three days a week; but sometimes she works only one day. However, when Saturday comes, I have to see to it that she gets money enough for a week's groceries. This is a haphazard financial arrangement; but, as I have already suggested, employing Negroes is distinctly a human problem. One is impelled to accept a certain personal responsibility for their support; and if this is bad for the bank roll, it is fine for the heart.

What I keep looking for among my workers is special aptitude, and I am finding it all the time. Indeed, it is tragic to come upon so much sleeping talent and at the same time to realize that little of it will ever find opportunity for development. Gentle little Flora has "a green hand." She can make anything grow. She loves flowers and bushes and trees. She hates weeds. She has not indeed mastered, as the officers of garden clubs master, the names of growing things. To her the Pride-of-India tree is just the "pindly-windly." But in her own way she can identify all growing things; and she seems by some happy dark magic to understand the individual characteristics of each. Any woman who will really work in a garden is better than a man at such business; for to her task she brings an instinctive feminine feeling for beauty and for order. Flora once said to me, "If you want anything to grow, you got to love it."

As with so many casual Negro sayings, there is in this one a deep poetic implication. I guess we may discover some day that the best way to make people flower is just to love them.

Negroes are very tolerant about matters financial—about money they owe and about money owed to them. Once I overheard this revealing dialogue.

"Iz you gwine pay me that dime what you owes me?"

"I ain't done say I ain't, iz I?"

"I ain't ax you if you ain't; I done ax you if you iz."

Expert in appeasement, they decided they had gone far enough; and from that delicate *impasse* they fell to gossiping.

Any employer who reads of my experiences may feel that he prefers his problems to mine; for my difficulties are unpredictable and continuous. Nearly all so-called labor troubles have money as the root of the evil. Strangely, the question of the exact amount to be paid is of small concern to me or to my Negro friends. If I did not give them work, they would have none. I am a poor man. I pay them all I can afford to pay. They know those things, and they are contented with what I can offer them. They are both sensitive and considerate. I always pay for overtime, and try also to pay according to the skill required. My highest paid man is my carpenter, Lewis Colleton. He is also my mechanic, my paper-hanger and my plumber. He can do anything.

As I have said, my problems are not such as an employer encounters in the ordinary plant, factory, mine, or business office. For example, my whole program of work can be upset by superstition; and when it comes to Negro superstitions, while I may not believe them, I am obliged to accept their belief in them.

I had a ten-acre field of oats to be cut; and the cutting of this particular grain ought to be very nicely timed. If it gets too ripe, it will shed badly when mowed.

"Prince," I said, "we must cut that field of oats on Monday. We ought not to wait another day."

I had to be away on Monday; but as I drove up the avenue in the moonlight that evening, I looked toward the oats field, expecting to see the mowed oats neatly stacked up. But the field of grain was still standing. I soon got hold of Prince to ask him why the work had not been done. He said that before he got up that morning he had heard an alligator bellowing far back on the wilds of the delta. That was a bad sign. It was no time in which to start anything. He thought he ought to wait until such portents had safely passed!

One day I had William Boykin at a very important piece of work in one of my gardens. He was transplanting camellias. Near where he was working stands a giant live oak. About ten o'clock I saw William furtively coming toward the yard. I knew that he was not merely after a drink of water. He sat down on a bench by the old kitchen. When I asked him why he had stopped work he would not at first tell me. He looked sick, but declared that he was not. I never try to compel a Negro to work; unless he works spontaneously, what he does will amount to little.

"Something scared you?" I ventured.

He nodded.

"Dat big owl," he said, with rolling eyes, "done been after me four or 'leven times."

Investigating, I discovered the nest of a great horned owl in the big live oak, and of course the mother, seeing William, was concerned about her nest. But William took her for what plantation Negroes call a Token; that is, a sign or symbol of something supernatural.

On one occasion the floodgate in my rice field was mysteriously blocked. Something was in the huge box deep under the water, that prevented the tide from flowing in and out of the field. At the onset of this trouble some Negro had unhappily suggested that the Devil himself was hiding in the trunk. This rumor soon became conviction and before I got the trunk working again, I had had to get a Negro from a neighboring plantation, his special qualification being that he had not heard the fearful rumor.

So accustomed is the Negro to having the white man set things straight that usually, instead of acting in an emergency, he will feel his duty done if he merely reports the trouble. I sent one of them to find a wild gobbler that I had badly wounded. The Negro found the great bird; it was unable to fly and could hardly stagger. But my man did not catch it. He walked back five miles to tell me that he had seen it. We never saw it again.

One of my friends employed a young Negro girl as a cook. Not long after she came, important company arrived for dinner. Family and guests were in the living room, awaiting those magic words, "Dinner is served."

At the door appeared Katie the cook.

"Miss Ethel," she said to the hostess, "de cat is up on de dinner table throwing down de dinner to de dog. An', Jedus, what a eatin'!"

Another characteristic that is both disconcerting and

[117]

expensive is the Negro's disinclination to tell you when a thing is going wrong. He reports only when it has gone wrong. Even Prince prefers not to mention trouble until it has become *un fait accompli*.

One of my deer hounds, glorified by being named Annie Oakley, was delivered of ten puppies. Sired by my Warcry, they were patricians. Being unusually busy for some weeks, I did not see the puppies, but kept asking Prince almost daily of their progress. About the time when they should have been six weeks old, I asked him how they were.

"Well, sah, the last one died today."

I had supposed that his previous optimistic reports meant that the survivors were still surviving.

On one occasion my work was held up by a strike. But a plantation strike is like no other strike in all the world. The demeanor of ordinary strikers is morose and truculent. When my Negroes struck, there was a perfect cascade of hilarious shouting and laughter. It happened when we were picking cowpeas in October. These are harvested in the pods, and the pickers are paid by the barrel. When this incident occurred, the pickers were all women—about twenty of them. As I came near, I could hear them having a great argument with Prince, but whatever the reason for their dispute, they were not only cheerful but positively merry about it. As I could not get the general drift, I drew Julia aside and asked her what was wrong. She pointed to the measuring barrel.

"This barrel's belly stands too big," she giggled.

Then I found that my foreman had substituted for a streamlined barrel, one of matronly proportions. Called upon to make one of these judgments of Solomon, I told my foreman to use the old barrel or to pay a higher rate if the swelled-front one was used.

But when it comes to judgments of Solomon, none is more difficult to pronounce than an answer to the question, Whose hog is it? In the rural South there is a stock law, but those who drive South know how cows and mules and pigs seem to think that the highways were built for them. Much stock roams loose; in the back country much of it is unmarked, and where such is the case, the big idea is to catch it and then claim it. One Negro came to me with a complaint that a white neighbor had caught one of his stray hogs. He said his hog had the "resolution mark," which I knew meant the mark that his people had used since the Revolution. Masterless swine invade my fields, and many of these are as wild as deer. Before laying down a barrage on them, I have to try to ascertain whether they might not belong to some of my Negro friends. If none is killed, they belong to no one; but as surely as I kill one, someone will claim it. I have gifts of hogs made to me, and it is well not to enquire too closely into their past. I do not know a more arduous existence than that lived by a roaming razorback. He is anybody's hog and even after his roamings have been violently terminated, dispute as to ownership of him continues. I once had to cut such a dressed carcass into four pieces in order to settle a dispute.

One difficulty I have that would be alien to the experience of the average employer is that when I send for two or three helpers, the whole Negro population of the plantation is likely to turn up. I have sent for two and have had twenty-four appear. As more than ninety per cent of the boys and men are now on relief work (and that is a whole story in itself), my work is done almost wholly by women and children. I hope the Government does not come after me for employing child labor; for example, I work little Mike. Both he and I are in considerable doubt as to what he does, but he is on the pay roll. One week he could not for the life of him recall anything that he had accomplished. At last his face brightened.

"I 'member now," he said: "I done carry a coco-cola bottle out of the cellar and t'row him in the ribber."

When my workers, summoned and unsummoned, descend on me, Prince and I have to go into a huddle to devise work for such a crowd. Regardless of the nature of the thing to be done, they all come armed with massive hoes; and it is a picturesque sight to see this army of dusky Amazons marching down the avenue toward the house. They always come laughing and singing and I find myself depending on their spirit for a morning uplift. To their credit let it be said that they will do anything I ask and sometimes they take a childish amusement at the tasks at which they are set. I believe they appreciate my rather desperate ingenuity in devising work for them.

One morning I asked Sam and Richard to make a dugout cypress canoe for me. They had never made one before and had never seen one made. They disappeared silently. Four hours later here they came down the road driving an old ox. He was hauling a gigantic cypress log that they had felled in the fetid swamp. Then, with ax and fire and adz they went to work; and by the next afternoon I had as pretty a ducking boat as you ever saw.

One day I had everyone settled at a task when two women appeared, apologetic for being "lated." For the life of me I could think of nothing for them to do. At last I said dubiously, "How about getting me some bootleg bricks?"

These two women did not demur. They got in a boat and all day long they made trips to the old illicit stills on the delta. By evening I had six hundred bricks stacked up on my landing. One of the most appealing human characteristics of plantation Negroes is that, whenever possible, they will try to make a lark out of their tasks. They do not like to work alone, but together, and will keep up a continuous teasing and banter. All the gossip of the community will be aired.

As I say, they will do anything, from heavy underbrushing to driving mules, from cutting wood to cleaning out rice-field ditches. In withering heat, tormented by deer flies and mosquitoes, in moldering morasses, in snake-haunted woods—there the Negro will toil and will be cheerful about it. I know I could not be. Sometimes one of them will convulse me with the casualness with which life and death are referred to. I was sitting with a group of them by the kitchen when one mentioned that he had seen some cottonmouth moccasins on the rice-field bank that all of them were compelled to cross in coming to work.

"Ain't no moccasin," said placid Diana with massive equanimity; "ain't nothing but a rattlesnake lashed at me this morning."

When the average employer of labor pays off on Saturday, he experiences a certain sense of relief that he has met his pay roll, and is able to dismiss that sort of thing from his mind for a week. But, after having paid off on Saturday, I always have to have a supply of cash on hand on Monday; for my employees will always want to borrow something on the coming week's work. I try to hold down these advances, but what is a man to do when he hears that "de baby ain't got no milk," and "Cousin Sue need some medicine bad," and "de tax man done run me down"?

Some of the appeals astonish me with their naïveté. One Monday early Ca'line came to me in great haste, and this was the burden of her song. So great had been her congregation's trust in her that she had been permitted to keep both the box and the key of the Skyrocket Resurrection Burial Society.

"I used the money," Ca'line told me, "because I needed it, and I knowed you would help me out."

Thus did I come near being a party to malfeasance. Of course I did as she expected: advanced her ten dollars. In this case I was really standing between her and the law. The Negro dreads the law partly because he does not understand (any more than many of us) its mysterious power. But he feels its majesty. Every employer of Negroes in the South is expected by his employees to stand between them and the statutes. A lot of my time and effort and some of my money go toward keeping my people out of jails and off chain gangs. They really behave no worse than we do, but they are singularly defenseless.

There is no employer who does not appreciate what it means to have an employee go the second mile. Among Negroes who are reputed to be highly gifted in inertia, I find a good many who do more than I ever asked or expected of them. For example, a little over a year ago I had an encounter with a bull alligator. From that experience I emerged alive but considerably battered. My wife, becoming anxious about my going into the wilds alone again, spoke privately to Prince, telling him that if he saw me disappearing anywhere, he should follow me. She meant that he should keep an eye on me until I got better. But to this day, whether by day or night, whenever I go walking alone, all I have to do is to glance over my right shoulder and there will be Gunga Din behind me, fifty paces, right-flank rear. This is the sort of loyalty that no money can buy.

One afternoon I was in an old rice field shooting ducks. They were lighting too far away, and I said to Richard, my Negro boatman:

"Richard, I wonder if you could not walk a little way around those ducks? They might then come to me."

I did not realize what I was asking, and did not know what had happened until he returned to me. More than a mile he had gone, swimming nine huge old canals; then he had come in on the ducks from that direction. On his return he took those nine canals in his stride, and when he reached me, mud and water from heel to head, he was all smiles because I had killed two mallards!

It does not often happen that an employer gets much of his philosophy of life from his employees, learning from them something of the high art of accepting gracefully the changes and chances of existence; learning also the magic of saving a situation by humor. I go to my Negroes for advice. I listen to their talk. Their grapevine telegraph is a marvel. Often, it seems to me, they tell me about things before they happen! And I am in lifelong debt to them for many of the things they say, without premeditation or any desire for display or effect.

Thus a favorite plantation prayer is, "O Lord, prop me up in all my leaning places!" One day in the back country I got confused about my roads. When I asked a Negro how to get to Charleston, he said: "Cap'n, if you really wants to go Cha'son, you mustn't start from here." What a universal lesson against making a wrong start in anything! Some of these Negroes went to France in 1917. Most vivid and memorable are their impressions of the big guns.

"Dem English," said one, "had a gun what could shoot twenty miles."

"Big boy," another answered, "dat ain't nothin'. Dem Germans had a gun, and all dey need was yo' address."

Said one Negro, lying in the sun in the happy agony of going to sleep, to another, in the same agony, but standing droopingly beside him:

"Boysie, if you wants to lie down, you got to make a effort."

I once spoke to an old Negro who was going to church. After a little talk, he said, with the unconscious native poesy that is his:

"Now I must go light my candle at His fire."

Somewhere between the juggernaut of a too-heartless materialism and my own disheveled and inefficient manner of handling workers there must be a happy medium. Experience seems to prove that an employer who takes an affectionate personal interest in his employees brings about

[124]

that noble and exciting combination of altruistic adventure and sound business. He will then experience more durable satisfactions than in getting work done. He will know what it means to be loved by those who toil for him. The genuine rewards of life are not usually in proportion to labor or to wages but in proportion to affection. Let all who speak of race questions be reminded that there are none. But there is always a human question, a heart question. And they who are called upon to maintain a fearful equilibrium will discover, I am sure, as I have here discovered at Hampton, that confidence in others, respect for them, concern and affection for them, regardless of their race or color, will go far toward establishing that spiritual balance which is the only genuine basis for peace. Whether it be with a man and his wife, an employer and his employees, any human being on the verge of conflict with another, love is the only solvent of all difficulties, and it is almighty. And to any employer with the vision to trust it will come the riches of returned affection in infinite.

Chapter 9

Floods at Hampton

I HAVE just described having to do with somewhat elemental human emotions here in my life at Hampton. I likewise have to deal with elemental nature. For example, I make it a practice to read the river bulletins every day. I should, for the great Santee River flowing past my door has, as I have said before, a length of three hundred miles. So though we may be having a drought, heavy rains to the north of me in western North Carolina, or in the Piedmont region of my own state, may bring down a flood. We may be said never to have a flood of our own; what we get is someone else's high water. When I see by the papers that the water in the river at Camden is twenty-five feet, or twenty feet at Rimini, I make such preparations as are possible against what the courts call an Act of God.

In the old days, when rice was planted here where I am, twelve miles above the mouth of the river, there were no great floods. I know that because the great dikes, built two centuries ago to harness the river—banks that were long entirely adequate—are now of little value. They are not high enough. The river goes higher than it did, and it does so in a short time.

Two things have caused this: one is the cutting of the forests to the northward, so that when rain falls, it races into the river, apparently intent on nothing so much as visiting me; the other cause is the fact that for years ditches and drainage canals have been dug, literally thousands of them, leading more or less directly into the Santee. We get plenty of water; but we do have warning of its coming. From Camden, for example, a freshet takes about a week to reach me, and thus I have time to get ready for it. The water in the river at my plantation may rise from five to twelve feet, this rise being boosted somewhat by the tide-water that is felt here, twelve miles from the mouth of the river.

But even the momentous flood has never come up to the foundation of my house. The reason is simple: those who chose the site for Hampton selected the very highest ground in that whole sweep of country. And it is rather remarkable that they did so, for when they built, they built in the wilderness, in the primeval forest. From the plateau on which the house stands to the level of the river at high tide the fall is about thirty-eight feet, and while I have seen a flood that covered all my growing crops to a depth of two or more feet, the ramping river, as the old song says, stayed away from my door.

To get an idea of the extent of country inundated by one of these floods, I may say that at such a time, if I paddle from my house straight across the two branches of the river and the intervening delta, the distance is close to four miles. Much of this country is naturally low and goes under quickly; but there are hundreds of miles of old banks and ridges that stand a moderate rise without being covered; however, a flood submerges all. After the water has reached its height, the full rise taking several days, it may stand for a day or so, and then slowly recede, bearing to the ocean a vast flotsam of old logs, sedge rafts, stray boats, chicken coops—indeed, all refuse that has been reached by the rising water and that will float.

On these natural or artificial supports, much wild life—chiefly swamp rabbits, king rails and cottonmouth moccasins are borne eastward to the coast and swept out to sea. But all do not perish there. Reaching the ocean, the river turns southward, and much of the drifting material with its living cargo that it has brought for many miles will be washed up on the beaches of the near-by coastal islands.

Every disaster brings its ghouls, and I have long observed the activity of birds of prey in the country immediately before an advancing forest fire. They are likewise active in a flood. Commonly, I see perhaps half a dozen bald eagles during the winter, but in a freshet I may see as many in a day, and lately I saw three, perched on the crests of low cypresses above the freshet tide and not more than fifty yards apart. They were just waiting for a king rail or a swamp rabbit to expose himself. Indeed, exposure is at such a time the great danger to wild life, for everyone of them is a born swimmer. But being forced out into the open is fatal to many of them. Eagles, hawks and owls take heavy toll of these refugees.

The kind of wild life one sees in a flood will depend largely on the time of year. It is in the winter, when the migrants are in my Carolina coastal country, and when the swamps are comparatively bare, that the observer has perfect, if distressing, opportunity to see hundreds of the furtive lurkers in the wilderness.

Some creatures are born aquatic; some are amphibious; some appear to belong wholly to the dry land. But in my own observation I have noticed that all wild creatures are born swimmers. For some reason, cats don't like water, but once they are in it, they look like experts in their own element. Furthermore, no wild thing ever seems to take a lesson in swimming. Once, in the time of a great flood, my boat passed under the top of a tree that was then some twenty feet above the raging tide. Out of that crest suddenly sprang the tawny bulk of a wildcat, an old brigand of the river swamps. Hitting the water with a resounding splash, he immediately began to swim the wild and affluent river. It surprised me to see with what ease and strength he stemmed the brute forces of that mighty current. A fox commonly avoids water, but he swims well. Although the occurrence is unusual, I have known one to take to water ahead of hounds, and to distance the pursuers in that way.

But if we raise the question of nature's champion swimmer, the place of honor must unquestionably be given to the otter. Of all living creatures, the otter is one of the most naturally attractive and naturally playful. As far as I know, it is for its size the strongest of all animals. It is also dauntless. I have seen one give a dog, many times its size and weight, the fight of his life. The otter's swimming, the acme of effortless grace, is like gliding tirelessly in every imaginable position at incredible speed. He is in the water, what Sonja Henie is on ice. He swims equally well on his back, his side, his stomach, and so little and perfectly controlled is his body that he often executes turns and performs stunts that would be the despair of an Olympic

[129]

performer. But the otter's grace and speed as a swimmer is never seen to best advantage unless one watches his performance under adverse conditions. Indeed, in any sport it is at just such a time that the real champion shows his mettle.

When the great freshet of 1939 occurred, with the waters some fifteen feet above normal, I went out in a canoe, trying to locate and possibly to rescue some of my stock that had been caught in the lowlands by the vast flood that swept down the river, submerging all in its path. The immense and gloomy power of this deluge seemed to have the whole river country in its grasp. Majestic in its sinister power, and in places more than five miles wide, the Santee, carrying even at normal flow the largest body of water of any river in the East, ramped stormily to the sea, carrying with it thousands of swimmers, tons of flotsam—rafts of sedge, old pine and cypress logs, whole years of debris from the mighty swamps to westward. The presence of all these obstructions in the water, and the speed at which they were being borne made swimming dangerous for anything. The wind and the waves were high; and the momentum of the flood had in it the irresistible power of an unleashed primitive force.

While a few of the fugitives from the wrath of the river had the sense and the hardihood to attempt to swim across the current to one or the other of the mainland shores, many of them were borne away on the floating refuse, and were thus swept seaward; many also simply swam with the tide, heading in the worst direction that they could have chosen. After a while, as I was holding my canoe in the lee of a cypress, uneasy about venturing forth on the tawny bosom of those wild waters, I saw near me a small animal swimming straight up against the tide. It was an otter. Of all this vast wild life community that I saw, he was the only one serenely composed, the only one I saw challenging that thunderous deluge. He seemed to know just where he was going and with his usual sportive cheerfulness he went to work. But floating directly toward him—really rushing down upon him, driven by the stormy wind—I saw the craggy skeleton of a huge tree, the dead branches sticking up at one end, the dead roots at the other. Massive in bulk, it could not have been less than eighty feet long. Floating broadside to the direction of the little swimmer's course, rocking and swaying crazily, it rushed down upon him. With a nonchalance that was almost comical, the otter, when he was within a few yards of the burly old giant, humped his back, dived, and a few seconds later reappeared above the log, swimming as if dodging death in a raging tide were just fine sport. For what we might call sheer gallantry in any circumstances that may arise, I hardly know the otter's equal.

In many ways the mink is much like the otter when it comes to swimming, but he is such a merciless predator that we cannot wholly admire his prowess, which is generally used for murder and marauding. Many of the crimes commonly attributed to the weasel really belong to the mink.

Perhaps the beaver might dispute the otter's claim of first place among all animal swimmers, but, while I admire the beaver as a most ingenious and sagacious creature, he is hardly beautiful. He seems to have a good deal of the rodent in him and that immense broad tail, while useful, is certainly not decorative. It is generally said, rather loosely, I think, that wild creatures do no voluntary work. But most of them work hard for the food they get, many of them risking their lives to procure it. And some work hard at building homes. Of the latter class, the most genuine laborer is the beaver, who hews down lumber of the proper size, cuts it into the right lengths, and with it— working in the water, too—constructs his dam and his house. Domestic animals are often made to work in water, and broken wild animals also; but the beaver is unique in his zest as a genuine toiler. Whether one pleases to attribute his engineering ability to instinct or to a kind of elemental reasoning power, no one can deny his industry and his unerring skill.

Practically every swimming animal can be overtaken by a man in a boat; even the otter can thus be overhauled. But he will never be caught, for he will dive.

The moose, the elk, the caribou and the reindeer—all are at home in the water; and when the caribou migrates, vast herds cross rivers and broad estuaries as if it were a matter of routine. On several occasions I have followed in a boat members of the deer family. Normal to top speed seemed to vary from four to six miles an hour, depending a good deal on whether the wind and tide entered the picture.

Among the most impressive swimmers are the reptiles and while there may be no true sea serpent, there are many sea snakes, deadly creatures but most beautiful swimmers. The great anaconda spends much of his time in the water. Reptiles somehow always seem to be more or less amphibious. Not long ago I captured a large king snake. Not wishing to harm this scourge of the venomous serpents, I nevertheless wanted to test his ability as a swimmer. I threw him from the shore about fifteen feet into the river. I knew he could swim. But what amazed me was the fact that he swam under water. As the water was clear, I could watch his black-and-white body until he came to the shore again, when, instead of showing himself, he merely sidled his head partly out of the water against the bank.

For a long time (until I found the number of my guests strangely decreasing) I kept about a dozen rattlesnakes, so that I could minutely study their habits. I tried out their swimming ability in my lily pond. Some of these serpents were from the mountains, where I doubt if they had ever learned to swim; some were from deep swamps, where they often had to swim. But all, on being thrown into the water, acted in the same way. The moment one would touch water, he would appear to inflate himself like an inner tube, so that he looked almost twice his normal size. So buoyed, he could lie at ease on the surface, could coil himself and could strike. Carefully I tested all these details. When on land the rattler crawls in a straight line; his track can always be identified. But in the water he lithely moves his whole body back and forth. His speed is far greater than it is on shore; indeed, most snakes in the water, including those that really belong on land, show a rather terrifying swiftness. There used to be a belief that

[133]

the rattler always holds his rattles above the water; for if he wets his bells they will not sound properly. I have seen some do this, but not all. I doubt if it is a regular habit. One of the most impressive sights I ever beheld in nature was a regal diamondback swimming the Santee River. Eight feet long, massive in bulk, his great spade-shaped head two inches across, he traveled in lordly fashion. When I first saw him, I thought he was a small alligator. As far as I have observed, the rattlesnake never dives.

Off the Carolina and Georgia coasts are the famous semi-tropical sea islands, in some instances separated from one another and from the mainland by several miles of water. In the mating season rattlers swim from one island to another. I was told by some of my friends who were fishing in a salt inlet that they saw a big rattler, going strong, halfway across a three-mile stretch of salt water. On such a swim, the greatest danger to the snake is the sea crab. Several of these ganging up on him from below can pull him under. One of four reasons will generally tell why a land creature takes to water: wanderlust, to escape danger, to get to better feeding grounds and the mating instinct. Of these, the last is the most compelling, and because of it wild things will take to the water that otherwise they would never enter. And they will not only go into the water, but they will perform stunts, make displays of themselves, to attract mates.

Perhaps the most eerie performer on or in the water is the water spider. While coots, partly supported by their wings above and by occasional lily pads below, seem to run on the water, the water spider really does it. He is only medium in size and when examined closely will be found to be a soft brown in color. But on and in the water he looks black. I do not know anything swifter in all nature than the speed of one of these magic insects over water. Sometimes the observer can see nothing but a faint blur. Moreover, he constructs with consummate skill a little silken diving bell, and in this mates, and rears his young beneath the water, supplying his oxygen needs by bubbles of air that he carries down lodged in the hairs of his body.

Occasionally a creature will swim that you never expected would. Discovering one day a wild turkey on a long ridge elevated above flood water—the only dry land for miles—I walked slowly after him to see what kind of an escape he would make. At the end of the ridge were several big trees with their feet in the water. The gobbler got behind these. It then occurred to me that I might catch him. I crawled for a hundred yards; I got up to the trees; with all the caution I could summon, I peered around their mighty boles. But the turkey had vanished. Looking off through the flooded swamp, I saw the gobbler swimming away. Those who have not seen such a performance might doubt its ever having happened. But Audubon records that he saw a whole flock of wild turkeys swimming the Arkansas River. I judge that under certain conditions a turkey decides that swimming is a wiser way to escape than flying. Chickens swim, but they seem to lose their heads in water, and try to fly in an element that does not permit them to take the air. Rabbits are beautiful swimmers, and raccoons are semi-aquatic. The squirrel is supposed to live only in trees and on the ground. I have seen one, sixty feet above the water, miss his jump and fall. It took him but a moment to recover his command of the situation, when he swam like a gray nymph for shore. I may be wrong in this suggestion, but it appears that all creatures with heavily furred tails dislike the water; such creatures as the cat, the fox and the squirrel. Of course, the otter has a furred tail, but that appendage is very different from a fox's.

Although we are taught by the Bible to have a low opinion of a hog, yet a pig is very smart, and in some respects, a very interesting creature. He is dogged, resourceful, has a good memory; if given anything like a chance, he is very cleanly, as all wild creatures are and he is a wonderful runner and an expert swimmer. Where I live there are more wild hogs than tame ones; but whether wild or tame, almost from the moment they are born, they take naturally to water. I have seen tiny pigs swimming a river half a mile wide; they were so little that I could hardly identify them. There is an old belief that a hog, in swimming, will sometimes cut his throat with his sharp front hoofs. But I have never known this to happen.

Hogs bred in a river country appear to be able to sense the coming of a flood. They have some far premonition of it. Sometimes on my plantation shores there will appear bands of wild hogs that immediately begin steam-shovel operations in my fields. A few days after their appearance we are likely to have very high water. This sort of premonition, common in animals, and savoring of a sense that we do not have, manifests itself chiefly when some kind of disaster threatens. Hogs are such powerful swimmers that

I never knew one to drown; if one does, he probably has been injured, or otherwise is out of condition.

It was late in February of this year that Rimini reported twenty-one feet, and I knew what that meant. I got my boats up high and dry; I opened all my rice-field trunks, so that the flowed field inside would equalize the pressure from the flood outside, thus saving my banks; and I got my stock to safety. Then I gathered together some feed to tide over the deer and turkeys until the waters subsided. And all the time I kept watching the river. You can be sure that the freshet has come when the water gets wild, murky, trash-choked, and when it is ebb tide all the time. There is also a peculiar noise, a continuous sibilant whisper, an urgent sort of rustling of the submerging marsh, with occasionally a roar from a breaking bank, or the sudden plunging of the flood through a high spillway. One hears, too, cries of surprise and alarm from wild things, and the air is charged with a feeling that elemental nature is on the rampage. It is.

Let us say that the freshet has arrived, and has flooded most of the banks and ridges and, of course, all the lowlands. It is a warm still day in earliest March that I venture out in a canoe. The yellow jasmine has begun to bloom. Myriads of migrating birds are on the move. To the leeward of windbreaks, tender green is showing. Life is awakening once more when this interruption comes.

I cross the south branch of the Santee and enter the timbered wilds of the delta, literally paddling through the woods.

I dare not put out a hand to touch a bush or to pick that

redbud maple. Not every one but almost every bush has, coiled upon it, or stretched prone on a low limb, or even festooning the top ten feet above the tide, a cottonmouth moccasin.

This is a good time to have a .22 rifle in the boat to make short of these truculent and deadly brutes. There on that drifting log, now stranded against those two big swamp cypresses, are a king rail and two swamp rabbits. And at the far end of the log is a moccasin. Floods make strange bedfellows.

It might well be wondered, when practically every living thing is his enemy, why the cottonmouth moccasin, one of the most dangerous of North American serpents, manages to survive in such great numbers in such a region as I am describing. Well, in the first place, he does not believe in birth control; in the second place, his habitat is such that he secretes himself easily; the fact that he is amphibious is likewise a little insurance policy for him; and finally, though living things in general dread him, few have the nerve to attack him.

To give a more accurate idea of their numbers, I might say that one has to be very careful about paddling the river edges in warm weather; for these snakes will drop from the bushes into your boat and they do not make winsome traveling companions. Once when we had a flood in September, I went to one end of a wooded bank on the delta, sending Prince around to the other end to walk toward me. We had lost some hogs and that seemed a possible way to locate them. The distance Prince had to walk was only about half a mile, and the bank was open. The warm waters of the flood were on either side, but the footing in the middle was dry.

I waited an hour while the mosquitoes crowded me. I got uneasy. I saw or heard nothing from Prince. I blew my horn and he answered, yet still a good way off. After a full hour he came; and as he approached I noticed that he carried a huge club, and that he was walking as a man walks who has just encountered a venomous snake. I asked him what had kept him so long.

He said that on that stretch of bank there was a big moccasin about every two feet; and that in order to make any safe progress, he had been obliged to stop long enough to kill every other one before taking another step forward.

Once when I was more zoo-minded than I am now, I caught about thirty in two hours, and I brought them home in my boat. About as many more escaped me. I well remember that the Negro who paddled me on that occasion manifested considerable doubt about my sanity and when I looked back to see whether he was really frightened, he was perched so far back on the stern of the canoe that he appeared to be sitting on air.

Fortunately for man, the moccasin rarely wanders more than a little way from the marshes, the gross river swamps, the fetid backwaters. If you go into such places you find him; but you will not meet him on the highland at any distance from the water.

Man, of course, is his natural enemy and little moccasins are killed by wild turkeys, who love baby snakes; by the great blue heron and other aquatic birds that have javelin-like beaks, and occasionally by hawks and crows. But big moccasins have few enemies in the wilds except the roaming razorback hogs. A razorback will go with grim gladness toward the biggest moccasin—or, for that matter, toward the lordliest diamondback rattlesnake—and just chew him up with the most comical nonchalance. Many young pigs are killed by snakes; and many half-grown ones are badly injured. But a mature hog has a tough hide, and under it no appreciable circulation. That fact accounts for this cool *savoir-faire* of the hog in approaching a deadly serpent, the very sight of which makes most men's spines distill into jelly.

Very near my house I have a big pond and occasionally moccasins get into it from the river. Not long ago I saw a loggerhead shrike hang a little snake on a dead twig of a holly tree in the yard; a short time later he repeated the performance. When I examined these baby reptiles—they were about six inches long—I found them to be true cottonmouths. Since then I have had a kindlier feeling toward my shrikes.

The loggerhead shrike, a bird about the size of a robin, is slate-gray and black in color. It takes up its abode in a certain tree and rarely goes far from home. While it has certain calls, it has no song. Curiously, while it is a genuine bird of prey and has the characteristic powerful beak of one of these predators, it has not correspondingly strong talons. Nature only half-equipped it for its task in life.

As I paddle deeper into the swamp, wild life becomes more abundant. I hear a tremendous splash ahead and see three deer swimming away from a pile of old logs on which they had been marooned. There are few better swimmers than the white-tailed deer; and at such a time my main object is to turn them toward the nearest highland. However, most of these have been bred in the marshes; they look different from ordinary deer; they have long spatulated hoofs; they take to the water almost like ducks, and they do not like to leave the delta, however flooded it may be.

From the direction that the deer have taken, I know that they are headed for the Pine Ridge, which is always the last land to be covered by a flood. Here grow a few primeval yellow pines, ancient cypresses, water oaks, giant hollies; and here the tall ridge rises, still above the freshet tide. Looking carefully I see those three deer are already on the ridge, and they have joined about ten others.

I go around to the northward, so as to turn them toward the mainland. Oh, they are wild, even in disaster, and it's a rather tragic thought that they don't hesitate to face this flood as man approaches.

Seeing something black and glistening, I discover some wild turkeys standing now like statues in obsidian. They look black because they are facing me; in this sunlight, if they were turned the other way, they would look a silver-gray. In some respects they are wilder than the deer; but they don't understand the meaning of a boat as well as the whitetail does.

There they go—both deer and turkeys: these off through the water, those into the high cypresses on the far end of the shadowy ridge.

[141]

I think it is better not to land. There are both copperheads and moccasins here, and perhaps a diamondback, all of which are in sullen temper, having been washed out of hibernation. At such a time, especially if the air or the water be chilly, a snake loses nearly every power except the blind instinct to strike. Here I see some of the fugitives: king rails, some Wilson's snipe, woodcock, swamp rabbits, gray squirrels. These last manage very well in a freshet, traveling great distances over the trees, but they, too, miss the chance to forage on the highland.

I follow those deer and keep them on their way to safety. . . . There they are, yonder, crossing that open stretch of water; they are still a mile from the mainland, but that fact will not worry them. They see me coming, and they'll keep on going until they climb the hill at Hampton. I'll keep away from the turkeys, for I have another plan for them.

It might be wondered whether in time of flood, it is safe to urge the dwellers on the delta toward the apparently safe but unknown country of the mainland. There is some danger for them in landing on strange shores. Once when, with my turkey call, I had lured a flock to a mainland hill, I saw a huge wildcat, possibly lured also by the call, craftily awaiting them. Deer seem bewildered in a strange land. They never take the regular runs that the "home" deer take. Birds like woodcock and snipe light right by the house; I have seen as many as fifty snipe around my lily pond. Creatures not so attractive also arrive at my back door: a sluggish alligator, drowsy and benumbed; wild hogs, as wild as deer, and vicious brutes; serpents, hoary with the age of the old delta.

I said I had other business with the wild turkeys; I think it's a pretty game to play. After experimenting with twenty-eight kinds of wood, and after working a good many years over the idea, I have at last perfected a turkey call. I call her Miss Seduction. She can fill a rival hen with furious jealousy, and can make a sophisticated old gobbler collapse emotionally. In fact, it isn't quite fair to take Miss Seduction into the woods. But when I take her on wild waters, she goes on an errand of mercy.

As I know the Pine Ridge will be covered, and know also that wild turkeys at such a time just sit in the trees, hungry and forlorn, it is my task to call them from tree to tree, coaxing them on until I can get them to a place where they can be fed. On the nearest high ground I have corn and rice spread for their repast. If they once find it, they will come back twice daily. And if only a few of a flock find the feed, they will get the others to come.

In times of distress I find it immensely heartening to observe how nature responds to trouble, how her children of a humbler order than man meet and overcome difficulty and disaster. After apparent ruin, nature always stages a recovery. She never shows fear. She is never hopeless. The glory of going on is immutably hers.

For almost every natural shock to which the human flesh is heir, I find a counterpart in nature. An old Negro once said to me, "Sorrow is common to the Race." In a deep sense sorrow is common to life. This same dusky philos-

[143]

opher remarked, "Unless a man is in trouble, his prayers ain't got no *suction*." Our faith and hope are perhaps never so fervent as when we are in distress.

To nature come storms, fires, floods, extremes of heat and cold, droughts. I stand in the lonely heart of a swamp from which a great flood has subsided. For a fortnight every plant and flower has been lost under the yellow smother of waters. The sun has hardly dried off the reeking death of the drowned swamplands before nature has set about her work of repair. Bushes that have lost all their leaves show hints of coming greenery. Serried ranks of marsh blades that have been mashed flat by the freshet tide are already recovering their upright positions. Everywhere there is an air of serenity, as if disaster were temporary. With nature ruin is transient. Life and resurrection of beauty are eternal.

A month later I revisit the swamp. Wild flowers are peeping out shyly from the dingy wreckage of the flood. Ferns of magic size are unfolding their mystical emerald fronds. A spirit of subdued triumph broods over all, a spirit of quiet rejoicing, which keeps singing to my heart, "Hope is stronger than fear; love is greater than grief; life is mightier than death; disaster is an incident of time. The shadows and rain of today will nourish the blossoms of tomorrow."

Chapter 10
Plantation Night

AT HAMPTON, nothing is more appealing to me than to be abroad during the night. Leaving the plantation house late in the afternoon, when magic begins to steal over the world, I wander down one of the old sandy roads winding between dewy and fragrant shrubberies and soon find myself in the heart of the lonely and beautiful wildwoods.

I leave behind the fields fading in the afterglow, the far glimmering reaches of the river marsh, the shouts and singing of the Negroes, the homely and subdued noises of a great farm getting ready to go to sleep. Before me gleams faintly the white, sandy road, leading, despite all the cynical views of the realists, into a true realm of romance; leading into the secrecy and hush and hidden bloom of the night; leading into the vast pineland country—pagan, aromatic, dim, full of voices, full of starry silences and strange with the glamour that day could never confer. It is a place alive with meanings, hints and whispers, with forms and shapes, tinged by starlight. To me, day has always been beautiful prose, clean and clear and delightful; night has been poetry, poignant and deep, full of those undertones that are attuned to reach the heart alone.

Into the winter twilight I walk while the gorgeous pageantry of the west fades in its brightness and, in fading, silhouettes the darkly momentous pines, standing like warders of the night. It is as if millions of warriors were drawn up at attention, after having been reviewed by their great commander, the setting sun.

My winter twilights are likely to be mild and of a stillness so profound that frequently I have heard the cries of wildfowl on the delta more than a mile away, and the talk of plantation Negroes almost as far through those slumbering woods. I stop on the edge of Summer Bay to take in the sights and sounds of that idyllic hour when night is beginning to fall.

Even to me to whom the sight of it is familiar, the peculiar attribute of motionlessness is strikingly noticeable. In summer in this pond, black bass can be seen jumping for dragonflies; alligators will swim with indolent strength on the surface or will bellow grimly from its dim borders, and patriarchal frogs will encircle the edges as if holding some mysterious council. But now all these are asleep. And the waters sleep with them. The wind that is swaying the pines has small effect upon this pond, for the many trees densely bordering its edge and standing here and there in the water are draped in gray moss that affords a delicate but effective barrier. Of these trees the "bald" cypresses are at once striking in their appearance. Their tops open and spread like the sequoia's, giving the appearance that they had grown to a certain level of ascent, above which no further growth save the lateral was permissible. These cypresses usually have the outer layers of bark stripped off, which gives the trees a yellowish color. This is the work of raccoons and fox squirrels that use this particular soft bark almost exclusively for bedding their holes. In seasons of great drought these ponds do not go dry. Nor have I known one to overflow.

But they are constant in loftier things than the level of their waters, for they change not in their beauty nor in their peace. A spirit broods here that is autumnal; it is rich and sad, full of haunting pathos. It has a tranquillity that seems entirely detached from life, and I can never look over the spiritual serenity of this place without imagining out of the remote and mysterious vistas between the mourning cypresses, the figure of Swinburne's Proserpine:

> Pale, beyond porch and portal,
>   Crowned with calm leaves, she stands
> Who gathers all things mortal
>   With cold immortal hands.

High over the trees pass great flocks of blackbirds; I mean companies of thousands, speeding toward the delta where they will roost in the marshes. Winnowing the air, small flocks of wood ducks pass, their strange shrill cries answered by the voices of their fellows in the lagoons and ponds. Soon the air will be alive with their dusky fleeting forms and vibrant with the music of their flute-like voices. Now, going in the other direction, a great spearhead of mallards drives westward, seeking, I know, harborage for the night in one of the great river swamps. With raucous grunts blue herons drift over with ponderous grace. I hear two in the heavens answering each other a half-mile apart. Out of the brakes, misty and glimmering, rise woodcock, that fly on whistling wings to coverts more alluring. Often, even in midwinter, at this mystic hour the woodcock sings his love song; indeed, I have heard a score singing all at one time. It is not the song that so fascinates as the performance that accompanies the singing; for here is a bird that, in the dim heavens high above the tallest trees, does wonders on his wings. So faint is the light that I can barely discern the performer as he stunts on his high trapeze. The flight is a mazy one; sometimes slow, sometimes dazzlingly swift; now up, now down; now along a straight aerial pathway. Delightedly he flies, ecstatically he sings, as if the coming of the night had suddenly liberated his soul. Even after the bird cannot be seen, the course of his flight can be traced by the thin sweet music of his wings and by his fairy song.

While it is continuing, other bird voices I hear, the good-night calls of white-throated sparrows, brown thrashers, cardinals. Wintering in the extensive shrubberies of the plantation, these birds do a lot of reassuring and comrade-to-comrade calling at sunset, as if they felt a communal interest in the safety of their fellows. Some of the sparrows sleep in the gray streamers of Spanish moss, and I have heard them calling with sleepy cheerfulness from their gently swaying cradles. The sky is suddenly darkened by a vast flock of birds; they are Florida grackles, boat-tailed grackles, red-winged blackbirds, cowbirds, and rusty blackbirds. They are going to roost in the marshes along the river. Now, in a funereal line, pass the black vultures; their powerful flight is very impressive. A covey of quail that has been scattered by some enemy begins to call together, the sweet querulous note of the old female having in it a human quality. Great flights of robins pass overhead, "changing swamps," or migrating from one feeding ground to another. Befitting this hour, from the depths of a gray swamp that has been moldering in silence, a great horned owl gives his far and melancholy note.

In a pine standing on the edge of the pond a wild turkey has gone to roost, though I neither saw nor heard him fly to his perch. He is rather dubious over something, for he will not settle on the limb but stands there rocking awkwardly, his long neck craned.

Wild turkeys have a regular range; sometimes this is of great extent, but they usually make a daily round of it. My strategy is to intercept them at a given place at a certain time of day. If I am where they are due at a specified time, they will hardly fail to be there, and on schedule. Like most living things, they hanker after the place where they were born, and unless greatly disturbed will commonly be found near the old hearthstone. I have known an unmolested flock to sleep night after night in the same trees, and sometimes on the same limbs.

As they go to roost in the twilight, and come to ground in the wan luminance of early daybreak, not many observers have studied closely their roosting habits. I wish I had even a devaluated dollar for every one I have seen go to roost. The whole performance has a good deal of wildwood magic about it, and is quite enough reward for a far ramble at dusk into the deep forest.

One evening near Fox Bay I was watching for deer to come stealing out of those shadowy thickets when suddenly very near to me and very loud, I heard a flock of wild turkeys calling. As I was hidden in tall broom sedge, and as the turkey does not apparently use his sense of smell for detecting his lurking enemies, these splendid creatures were completely off their guard. They were not calling strayed members of the flock. They were just having a twilight frolic before going to roost. They kept dashing at one another in mock anger, stridently calling all the while, almost playing leapfrog in their antics. Their notes were bold and clear, and some that they gave would defy imitation; indeed, had they given none but the queer tones, and had I not seen them, I should have been unable to identify the callers. For about five minutes they played on the brown pine-straw floor of the forest, then, as if at a signal, they assumed a sudden stealth and stole off in the glimmering shadows. I stole after them. In a few minutes I heard them flying up to roost; maneuvering nearer, I had the pleasure of watching sixteen take to the trees.

In flying up they make little noise until their great wings strike the limbs and branches of the trees in which they alight. That sound, once identified, can always be recognized again. Contrary to general opinion, turkeys rarely roost high, and they prefer evergreens to bare trees for obvious reasons. I have found them chiefly in the dense tops of young yellow pines, not over forty feet high, and I have, in the moonlight, walked under wild turkeys roosting not more than twenty feet from the ground. When a wild turkey decides to sleep in a bare tree he usually makes some attempt to camouflage his presence by selecting one that has in it festoons of moss, bunches of mistletoe, or old squirrel nests. In the eerie visibility of oncoming night it is often difficult to distinguish a wild turkey even in a bare tree. I usually do so by looking for what does not naturally belong there. The two best features for identification are the long snakelike head and neck moving against the pale darkening sky, and the excessively long tail, which is more conspicuous when the bird is roosted than at any other time.

When flushed from the roost at twilight or at night, turkeys invariably alight in other trees, usually bare and usually absurdly near by. When flushed at daybreak, they commonly alight on the ground. In a lifetime of observing them in their native haunts, I never knew one to alight on the ground at night. This behavior shows the great bird's abiding respect for foxes and wildcats. In a swamp at dusk I have made a wild turkey fly five or six times; always would he alight in a bare tree, and never did he go more than a hundred yards. But I have seen a wild gobbler, scared from a tall pine in the daytime, tower to such a height and take such a course as made me certain that he would not come to ground short of a full half-mile.

While not nocturnal in its habits, one of the dwellers of the pinelands that is most restlessly active at twilight is the fox squirrel, a most beautiful and graceful creature, three times the size of an ordinary gray squirrel. While the very last roses are fading from the giant oriel windows of the west, moving against the sky on one of the tinged spires of a water oak, a fairy shape, shadowy in the shadowy air, moves with infinite litheness and grace along the dark limbs and through the bright foliage. Only the swaying of a branch beneath his weight betrays his presence. From the water oak he jumps to a dead tupelo, and this he climbs to the very top, where he perches high above the woods, his lissome form silhouetted against the sky. His extraordinarily long tail is draped over his perch with unintended grace. Why he goes to that high station at such an hour I cannot tell. Is it not because he loves beauty and gains from a sundown some of the same delight as is then ours? It is my persuasion that wild things love beauty. Our love of that kind becomes articulate in poetry, music, painting and sculpture; theirs, though inarticulate and possessed in a minor degree, is none the less genuine. There the fox squirrel sits, gazing out over the vast sea of pines. He has found nothing to eat; he has no tryst with another squirrel; he is just pausing to enjoy life. And my enjoyment in watching him is akin to his pleasure in surveying things from a little private throne in the wildwoods.

To one who has been out much at night in the wilderness, there are perceptible distinct degrees of darkness, and there are varying kinds of silence. During the twilight and the dusk there is much subdued activity of wild things preparatory to retiring. Then the woods are suffused with lilac, orchid and rosy lights. The transition from day to night has the quiet majesty that we associate with the eternal cosmic processes. Day dies in beauty, and night awakes in loveliness. The effect of this immense serenity on the human spirit cannot but be beneficent. At such a time I feel the touch only of the things great and immemorial, only the mightier movements of nature, only the stars and the seasons, only winds and rivers and stately trees, only life and love and death. The pinelands at night reconcile me to all that has been or may be; there I become an intimate of eternity, a joyous living soul, a child of God once more. As the great forest composes itself to sleep, so the human spirit in that environment comes to a stillness of ecstasy, accepting life as a privilege to be in communion with beauty and with ancient order and with the eternal rhythm of creation.

About a half-hour after the last of the amethystine light has faded from the west, a profound silence settles over the woods. All diurnal things are at rest, and the nocturnal things have not yet freely begun their roaming of the dim country of the night. It is at this time that the air is most richly perfumed with the dewy fragrances arising from wet leaves, damp pine needles, misty myrtles. Through the plumed and purple tops of the pines the starlight steals wildly yet softly. From broom sedge and white sand and warbling water clean aromas exhale. It is the hour of nature's brimming chalice.

After a while the woods begin to be full of subtle movements of the wild creatures; there are subdued crackings of dry branches and twigs; there are sinuous brushings aside of bay bushes and gallberry plants; there are wary footfalls, almost soundless, yet audible. The barred owls and the great horned owls hoot, scream, and weirdly intone their occult callings and challenges. I hear an old foraging raccoon grunting in the bosky green darkness of a watercourse. All about me there is the sense of a host of shadowy creatures, near, yet invisible; intensely wild, yet close to me. I identify them by the little noises that betray their presence and their identity. In the brightening starlight I can barely discern a few of these. That dusky form, looking almost black in the white road, is a gray fox; that stolid lumbering

[153]

shape that looks almost white against the dark pine straw of the forest floor is a 'possum, a strange Dickens-like character in the community of wild nature that just wheedles his way through life. Little elfin noises in the bushes and grasses and among the fallen pine cones tell me that the wood rats and wood mice are frolicking and feeding. It is strange, but one of these humblest rodents makes almost as much sound in moving about at night as does a deer, the noblest game of this country. He is the very spirit of the night: secret, star-wild, vanishing. I know now that deer are abroad in the dusky woods within easy sight, if it were day; but they are invisible, and the few sounds they make seem but a part of the wide mysterious whispering of the forest. Yet I know that I shall see some of them, for that conflagration in the east, where a thousand pines are beginning to burn, is the rising moon.

From my station I move up a little woodland hill, where the forest is open and park-like. On my way, wild things get my scent, and scuttle or dash softly or crash away, the manner of their flight being determined by their size and their temperaments. By the time I reach my new position, moonlight is flooding the woods, and that mystic radiance has both a revealing and a concealing power. Here I will sit on a pine stump until deer come by me in the moonshine, as I know they will; for over this little rise runs one of their favorite paths. While they wander and stray a good deal to feed, they have standard highways; and from plantation records that go back as far as the year 1686, I have reason to know that the wild deer are now using the same pathways through the woods of home as they did three centuries and a half ago; and likely for ages before the coming of the French Huguenots.

Moonrise in the pinelands is the witching hour, when every scar is magically healed, when every object, however obscure and mean its aspect by day, is wrought to virginal marble by an all-forgiving wand, is statued in lily-white stone. The beauty of the moonlight has always seemed to me not so much a thing in itself as its transforming and transfiguring power. In that it is like love.

I have a long wait, but who will not wait amid deepening peace and increasing loveliness? At last they come: two fairy shapes, silent, elusive, beautiful. The mild night air is drifting from them to me, so that they do not detect my presence. Here are two great silver stags with silver horns, moving with unposturned grace through a silvery world. They pause, as if posing for an urgent picture. Nearer they come, and I notice that at certain angles in the moonlight they are almost invisible; at others they are vividly visible. Past me they glide like spirits of the wilderness, having all the meaning connoted by the night, by stillness, and by the unwearied charm of nature. Into the silver silences they vanish.

In these pinelands there formerly were many homesteads, now not only deserted but so completely disappeared that their sites are marked by nothing but a few live oaks that seem memorial. The mockingbird is not usually a dweller in the woods, but often a pair will be found on one of these oaks, the trees and the singers continuing the tradition of former human habitation. As I leave my station to turn homeward, in the lonely moonlight I hear a mockingbird filling the tender silence with ecstatic music. On quivering wings he rises, singing in his flight. It is to this melody that I walk back to the plantation road, reaching it as the real deep night comes on. To me there is something strangely unexpected in hearing a mockingbird choiring in the pinelands, something as disconcerting as a baby's sigh, as if I had not really understood all that was in a heart that I thought I knew.

Yes, romance is in the pinelands, often when dawn spreads over them the streamers of her wide effulgent banners, often when those solitudes are shaggy with twilight, but most, I think, when night there ascends her lonely fragrant throne. For then the soul like some shy flower, opens wide under the light of stars. . . . Night in the pinelands has brought me great happiness.

Chapter 11
Lady of My Dreams

O N ENTERING Hampton, one sees on the right,
standing in the open field, a giant live oak that must
have been overlooking that landscape for more than three
hundred years. There are other great oaks about the place,
but this one, close to the gate, has always had for me something of the personality of a faithful sentry.

But for the glimmering pillars, he has veiled
    The house from view. Tall, twilight-dim he stands,
    The guardian of lustrous summer lands,
In glory of his emerald armor mailed.

As when a boy his stalwart bulk I see,
    The proud and ancient sentinel! His form
    Has gathered grace from sun and power from storm.
Lone in the dusk he looms tremendously.

At sight of him, my heart is filled with joys:
    My monarch oak is standing, massive, grand . . .
    Ah, no mere oak he is! I understand
The meaning of this steadfast giant's poise;

This vast glad strength; this purpose calm and deep,
    This brow heroic that with stars confers;
    This rooted hardihood; this light that stirs
The foliage in its bright aerial sleep:

Lo, he had waited my return so long!
  A thousand dawns of disappointment came;
  Vainly he saw a thousand sunsets flame;
But ever he was watchful and was strong.

While I in far forgetful paths would roam,
  My oak stood sure, devotion's faith to prove;
  Pledge of the proud eternity of love,
Powerful warder at the gates of home!

Nor has such a tree been the only guardian, during my absence, of the Lady of my Dreams. Ancient Negroes kept the watch: Old Lewis, Gabe, Galboa; with a faith and a patience akin to those of nature herself, they stood by, waiting for my return. They do not, as we do, have to learn to accept life. They take it as they take the weather: with joy, if there be cause for rejoicing; with quiet resignation, if that is required. I would not take a good deal for what they have taught me—not the least thing being an equanimity that can come only from grace of heart.

Particularly I think of Galboa, who spoke more African than English. He had been a plantation fisherman, and brought to his task his almost occult knowledge of nature and her secrets. He was the only man who ever caught the lordly Susquehanna salmon in the Santee River. I remember once taking a bird dog to him to be broken. With this dog of somewhat dubious social background, I had been able to do nothing. When next I saw Galboa, couching his appraisal in large and philosophic terms, he said of the dog, "Cap'n, ain't you know dat *nothin' eber can be done about a fool?*"

These old Negroes are living links with the distant past,

but there are other reminders that Hampton is a place that has seen much of life. My questing for buried treasure continues, and is rewarded. Coins are found; and, to my surprise, the prevailing one is the Spanish half-dollar of silver. I found one of 1720 in perfect condition. A medal of President Lincoln, dated 1864, turned up. On one side are pictured marching armies, on the reverse, the bust of the President, with the legend, vote for Abraham Lincoln. No doubt this medal was lost by a Federal soldier when a party of them landed from a gunboat near the mouth of the river toward the close of the war.

I have an aunt who is now ninety-three years old. She first saw Hampton when she was a child of six. Not long ago she delighted me by saying that the old place is now more beautiful than she could ever remember having seen it. I believe the reason for that is the wide underbrushing I have done. Where the open spaces end and the woods begin, I have hundreds of dogwoods and Judas trees blooming. I have felled scores of great trees, letting in the light. Instead of seeing a smother of jungle-like thickets growing up to the very doors, one can look through to the river, can see the majestic boles of the live oaks and giant hollies and, of course, can obtain a much clearer view of the house itself.

When I first came back, it was sagging in places and it had not been painted in a generation. Now everything has been done to restore it without changing it and it gleams under its four coats of white paint. It is no unusual thing for visitors to tell me that in its simple dignity it is the most impressive home they have ever seen.

[159]

In this climate, until recent years, no one ever had a furnace. Now, certain country homes are so heated; but as the winters are mild, a furnace is likely to be of dubious benefit. Every room in Hampton has a big fireplace and all our heating is from open fires. Fortunately we have on the place the greatest abundance of wood, and of kinds that are especially good for burning. Our big backlogs are usually of seasoned live oak and we use as fillers ash, hickory, scrub oak and water oak. All the kindling is done with lightwood, which comes from trees that have been worked for turpentine. So resinous is this wood that at the touch of a match it flares into flame. I do not think a lump of coal has ever been burned here.

Many visitors to Hampton are amazed that we have no electricity. I suppose that at some time we may put it in. But for the present we manage very well without lights, the radio and refrigeration. We use lamps and candles entirely for lighting. Many of these candles are held in the old "storm-shelter" type of holder; one in particular is notable as it is wrought in decorated brass.

A small room at the back of the house, immediately behind the dining room, now serves as a kitchen. We use a range but the fires are all of wood. It is my practice to take two or three days off in the autumn and saw enough scrub oak for stove wood to last the entire winter. When Sue, who cooks for us, begins to run short of wood, she takes it as a personal affront from old Gabe Myers, one of her ancient boy friends, and, as you can imagine, her disapproval can put more vitamins into Gabe than all the doctors in the county.

People often ask me how we live at Hampton. I mean that, for all its beauty and romance and history, life there requires what life requires everywhere: food and drink. We are only fifteen miles from good stores. We raise on the place corn, peas, some rice, sweet potatoes. I have a regular system of kitchen gardens from which we get green peas, lettuce, carrots, spinach, asparagus, strawberries and many other vegetables. I like to take care of these small crops myself. We raise beef, pork, chickens, ducks and turkeys. I am now experimenting on raising half-wild turkeys from a totally wild gobbler. This strain is much more hardy than the domestic one is. Throughout the game season (which runs for nearly six months) I can always supply the table with game in season— venison, wild turkey, quail, wild ducks. So wild are my woods and so plentiful is game that my wife often says to me, with real faith in her voice, "We have nothing for dinner."

I then take a gun or rifle, and stroll forth to look for dinner. Sometimes I do not have to go farther than the front gate.

Deer at night come up to the front gardens. One morning early I saw a buck in the back yard. When he saw me he made for the river, which he swam. The island he gained is a part of Hampton. Absolutely wild, it is full of game. I never hunt there. If a deer or turkey escapes to that sanctuary, it is never followed. I think every property owner, if he permits hunting at all, should set aside a part of his estate as a game sanctuary. States do so now, and if individuals did so, there would be genuine hope for the future of our wild life.

It might be imagined that this would be a lonely life, but too many people come here to see Hampton for life ever to lag. They do not come to see me—except occasionally—but to get a view of this example of the Georgian country house of colonial times. In a single afternoon I have had more than thirty strange cars come to my doors. Strangers are welcome. Since they evidently love beauty and history and antique architecture, I like them to come. And for all our remoteness, and despite the fact that wild creatures roam all around us day and night, I can always hear on the great three-mile Santee Bridge that spans the delta only two miles to the eastward, the roar of traffic on the Coastal Highway. Most of it goes to Florida and returns from Florida. Though I do not dislike Florida, I think most tourists go too far in their travels. The winter climate here is like that of October in the North.

It is indeed a gay cavalcade that visits Hampton. One day a darling Dresden-china lady introduced herself as "Miss Alcott—one of the Little Women." Although I am far inland, one day three admirals came. Nor is the plantation inaccessible even to English nobility: for Lord and Lady Ashley-Cooper and Lady Duff-Cooper came to pay their respects to the Lady of my Dreams. People from all states come to see what America once was. They come in cars that look like new locomotives, and in cars that hiccough and reel.

What is it they want? They have altered for the better my opinion of humanity. The human heart loves instinctively old, authentic, home-bred things. It comes searching.

Without feeling that any of their yearning can be fulfilled by me, I know that Hampton is, in part, an answer to some of their mortal longings, even as she is to mine.

Occasionally visitors come on what they believe to be a mission.

One day while sitting at dinner, I saw three people walking to the house from the gate—a distance of more than a quarter of a mile. I met them when they reached the front porch. The man of the party introduced himself as a major, but he wore no uniform. With him was a woman who certainly was beautiful and looked intelligent. Bringing up the rear was a stalwart young man of Neanderthal or football aspect.

Ushering them in, I began to talk of Washington and Marion, La Fayette and Tarleton. But they were not in the least interested.

Finally the major said, "We could not presume to walk up to this house."

I had no answer ready for that.

"We did not come here," he went on, "to hear history or to see this home. We came to see you. We are from Illinois."

Having never committed any crimes in Illinois, I was puzzled. Uneasy, I backed a few steps toward the hall doorway, near which I keep my gun standing.

After several more minutes of deepening unrest, the man addressed his wife (I suppose they were married).

"Shall I tell him?" he asked, with a dramatic emphasis that gave me the creeps.

"Yes, Oscar," she said, "tell him."

She smiled, but her eyes looked unfathomable things at me.

Said the major, "We have come here on a great mission. We have come to announce that Christ is coming—is now on his way. There will be twelve new apostles; and you are to be Number Eleven. Of course," he hastened to explain, "you could not be Number One, for I am Number One. We are on our way to Danbury, Connecticut, to notify Number Twelve. As soon as he is notified, Christ will arrive."

As he spoke, I saw in his eyes the sad and glittering light of insanity. What really disconcerted me, however, was the way in which his intelligent-looking wife kept energetically agreeing with everything he said! I decided it would be wise to play along with her. Therefore when he asked, "Haven't you felt this coming on?" I replied with specious prevarication—"Yes, all winter."

Was she a nurse and was the young husky a keeper? I never discovered.

For some time after this adventure it was all I could do to keep my friends from calling me Number Eleven.

But I have other comforters for what might be loneliness, than the coming of strangers and listening to alien traffic. Old friends come to see me. I never have any trouble with poachers, for the most renowned of this county are all my boyhood friends. One drove in the other day and gave me a hunting horn—just for old times. The very wealthy owners of great estates—for I live on the border of a colony of multimillionaires—have been most gracious to me, and often come informally to visit this rustic native. And I am privileged to go right into their exquisite homes with my hunting clothes on. That means much to a man who, when he puts on a dress suit, looks alarmingly like a mule peering over a whitewashed fence. The work that the wealthy men from the North have done in restoring the desolate and abandoned plantations in the coastal regions of the South is about as fine as anything that has come to my view.

Humble people come to see me—Old Gabe, for example. With him I have hunted for forty-three years. He is so black that when he leans against a burnt pine, you can't see him. Too old to hunt now, he is not too old to negotiate a loan.

"Cap'n," he said to me not long ago, "when is you gwine to sis me wid dat sissance what you gwine sis me wid? I did have a little pig on the delta. Now, if so be dat alligator don't catch him, and if so be dat I can catch him, I will give him to you sometime if you will len' me two dollars now."

Old Gabe got his money. That was to be expected. And I got my pig, which really was not in the picture at all.

I have three sons who love this old place just as I do. Now, if I can leave them Hampton, with some of its ancient dignity and beauty wakening to a new radiance, it ought to make up for the stocks and bonds that I do not have to leave them.

There has been much said about the work done by my Negro helpers and by me. But the real charm of the house is the interior, and the supreme task of decorating the many rooms has been accomplished by my wife. She has also planned the gardens. A loving comrade in all my adventures at Hampton, she has been my mainstay. Without her I might have done something, but probably it would have been wrong.

Already I find the compensations great. For the first time, almost, in my life I am not timed by bells. I awake to the drowsy calls of the plantation birds. I am close at last, after nearly half a century in a highly civilized society, to the elemental things I love: To the deep wildwoods all about me; to the river and its eternal tides; to the plantation Negroes, whose only true philosophy is that life was given us for enjoyment; to the fields I roamed as a boy; to the ancient hearthstone.

The days at Hampton are full of friends, of work, of hope. All about is a sense of calm, of joyous relaxation. The quail call, and the doves from the oaks; the wide fields sleep in the sunlight. There is here a gentleness that suggests what life can be; that in the realm of the heart, inglorious is the victory of might. There is something that persuades one to accept quietly life's stillness and its song. Only by such reconcilement can we find an answer to life's longing. Here, in this deep harbor of eternal dreams, the spirit finds sanctuary and is able, untormented by life's badgerings, to meditate on the mystery all about us. The calm of the natural world must be the peace of God.

Sometimes when I stand on the porch in the moonlight, I imagine that I can see the Santee Indians flitting from oak to oak; then Tarleton's Redcoats thundering up the avenue; then Francis Marion and his partisans stealing in by the back door to devour the "leavings" of a plantation dinner; then the chariot of General Washington, coming up in state, somewhat creaky for need of axle grease. And I see Judith Serree, my far ancestress, whose father built Hampton; and I think of the book I have, inscribed "Judith, her book, Hampton, 1730." And I realize that I, too, am but a visitor here in this stately home. I am, therefore, trying to be a considerate guest.

[168]

Hampton, built in 1730, is located in the coastal country of South Carolina, forty miles northeast of Charleston.

Prince, Sue Alston's son and foreman of Hampton.

Harrietta House, built by the author's great-grandparents for their daughter, Harriott.

This handsome bed is an example of the furnishings at Hampton.

A corner of the master bedroom in which the ancient wallpaper has been re-produced.

An enormous brass lock and key on one of the doors at Hampton.

A magnificent set of Shakespeare from the library.

One of the most beautiful of the parish churches of early America is St. James, Santee (built about 1760).

In 1791 George Washington advised that this live oak growing near the house be allowed to stand.

Eight great pillars support the front porch.

The panel above the fireplace in the ballroom is more than seven feet wide.

The fireplace is faced on either side by Delft tiles in color.

The scenes vary to suit every taste from Bacchanalia to Biblical pictures.

Negroes kept the watch with a faith and patience akin to those of nature herself.

The old kitchen is a building entirely separate from the house but complementary to it in design.

Sue Alston, guardian angel of Hampton.

Turkeys are always plentiful at Hampton.

Negroes hull their home-grown rice as in the old days

Gentle Flora has a "green hand." She can make anything grow.

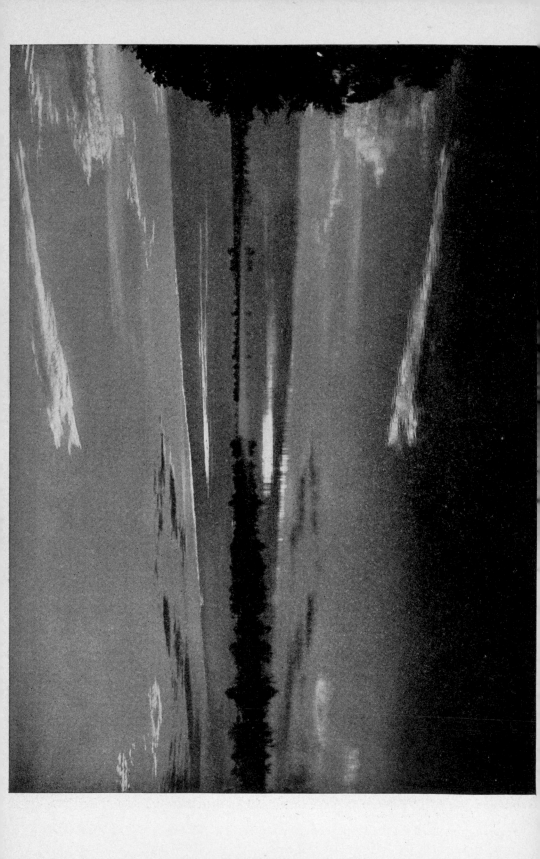

In springtime Negroes are torn between a desire to go fishing and a desire to start a crop.

Regardless of the nature of the thing to be done, all come armed with massive hoes.

They do not like to work alone but together, and keep up a continuous banter.

Old Gabe with whom the author has hunted for forty-three years.

The house, restored, gleams under its white paint.

"I, too, am but a visitor here; and I am trying to be a considerate guest."

Archibald Rutledge with his deer hound.